SIMPLE INVESTING:

The Dividend Investing Strategy to Grow Your Passive Income

MoneyByRamey.com

Matthew Ramey

A MoneyByRamey.com Book

About MoneyByRamey.com

MoneyByRamey.com was formed in May 2017 with one goal in mind: to Teach Financial Freedom to the Universe!

We teach anything and everything money, with the main focus being on building up passive income sources to achieve greater financial and time freedom.

On the site, you can live track the MBR dividend portfolio, use our dividend calculator to discover forward income on various stock positions, and improve your overall financial acumen.

About Ramey

Matt Ramey is an avid reader, writer, investor with vigorous entrepreneurial spirit.

He owns and operates MoneyByRamey.com, where he writes on his journey towards building up Active and Passive Income, while teaching others to do the same.

In his spare time, he enjoys reading, writing poetry, and playing various sports especially basketball.

Other Books By Ramey

Simple Budgeting: A Minimalist's Guide to Setting Up Your First Budget

Acknowledgements

To my Family, for always supporting and loving me.

To my Friends, for the same.

To those have come before me, and paved way for the inventions of today.

To those who will come after me, building upon what we have done.

To My Readers:

Thank you for being AWESOME!

A special thanks to you for purchasing this book on dividend investing. I trust that you will find the information in the following pages useful to you in your Financial Freedom journey, especially when it comes to investing in dividend paying stocks.

If, after reading this, you are thrilled with the information contained within, please visit Amazon.com and leave a review. Reviews help my books to be seen by more people and give me feedback on what is positive about this book so that I can write more materials just like it!

Or if you have feedback that you'd like to share with me directly, feel free to email me at

Ramey@MoneyByRamey.com

or leave a comment on the website,

www.MoneyByRamey.com.

Thank you and happy investing!

Best,

Ramey

Before we get started, here are a few legal items to get out of the way!

"Go as far as you can see; when you get there, you'll be able to see farther."

JP Morgan

Table of Contents

Introduction

Welcome and thank you for taking the time to read this book on dividend investing. My sincere hope is that you will gain actionable knowledge by reading the information contained within these pages.

The chance to share a bit of what I know and have learned through my experiences humbles me beyond belief. I am excited to be your partner in your journey towards the ultimate end goal: Financial Freedom.

Although I wrote Simple Investing for individuals who have a firm grasp of financial and investing concepts, my goal is to make the information easy enough to understand for anyone looking to begin their investing journey. It is my desire that everyone can learn from the information contained within these pages.

Per usual, my strategy in all aspects of life is to put the concepts I teach and write about in the simplest terms possible. I do not believe we need to over complicate things and in fact, in doing so, we miss out on the essence of life: simplicity.

For those of you that are ready to learn the world of dividend investing, read on! For those of you just beginning your journey into investing - specifically dividend investing - view this quest as a long winding path upon which you are now traveling; at the end of this destination lies our ultimate goal - Financial Freedom.

Remember that any type of investing is fraught with risks and dividend investing is no exception. No matter what camp you are in - beginner, expert, or somewhere in between – make sure that you go into your investments with eyes wide open as to the risks and pitfalls.

As with any investing strategy, you could gain money and you can lose money. Take action accordingly and with full responsibility of where you are heading.

My dividend investing strategy was developed through much trial and error over a period of 15+ years. I have been on "both sides of the proverbial coin"; I have experienced lost capital, amazing appreciation, and stagnant performance. I have seen it all.

Throughout these experiences, I have honed and refined my processes all in an effort to find what works for me as an individual investor. Going through all of those scenarios, I have finally arrived at a strategy that I feel comfortable executing on a day-to-day basis.

Even though I have been refining my overall investing strategy over many years, it was five years ago that I became fully plugged into the dividend movement. I stumbled upon a blogger who wrote straightforward posts and chronicled his journey towards living off his dividend income.

While he sold the blog and now lives in Thailand, I am thankful for his contributions and effects on my life. Because of his candor and open sharing of his life and journey, including posts where he showed the exact value of his portfolio and dividend income, I gained motivation and realized that I too could accomplish the goal of living off passive income that is generated through dividend paying stocks.

I still remember reading his posts and working to understand how I could duplicate his progress.

With each position he added, I made attempts to understand the strategy and structure behind the method. Though I was learning so much, I did little in the way of execution.

I was stuck in the "I wish that was me" thought process as I saw him building up his net worth and dividend income. At the time, I had a small dividend portfolio, but I was clearly not yet ready to make the push into investing on my own as a full strategy endeavor. Certainly I had made headway, but it seemed to be in such small increments that I felt like I really was not beginning at all.

At the heart of things, I was scared.

"Scared of what?" I would ask myself. There seemed to be many things I was scared of: choosing the wrong to stocks, losing capital through poor decision making, looking foolish in front of others who knew of my self-investing dividend strategy, screwing up my future cash flow, not having the 'right' plan, etc.

There seemed to be an endless stream of reasons to not do the thing.

Other questions continued to roll through my mind:

- Could I even achieve Financial Freedom?
- Is this dividend investing strategy something that can really work?
- Shouldn't I just stick with traditional, passive, target-fund investing strategies like everyone else?
- What would my life look like when I achieved Financial Freedom?
- What would I do with all of my extra time?
- What would my friends and family members think of me?

These questions were certainly on the forefront of my mind, lurking, lingering, and making me question the path forward.

However, somewhere deep inside of me, I knew that I needed to continue on the path forward. I needed to gain the knowledge to begin investing on my own as well as transition my thinking from a negative-oriented, scarcity mindset to a positive-oriented, abundance mindset.

This caused a change in the flow of my thoughts. Rather than think of all the reasons not to do the thing, I began to reflect on all the reasons to do the thing.

From this, there arose a new ultimate question: it was no longer 'will I achieve' freedom but 'when will I achieve' Financial Freedom?

From this a new question arose; "Why am I here and what is my life's purpose?" Though I am unsure if I will ever truly know the answer to this question, I am confident that my search for Financial Freedom will allow me the chance to explore it in greater depth.

In the end, I believe this is what we are ultimately all after - a chance to explore our life's purpose in this brief time we are allotted on this earth.

Though I am continually answering and refocusing my life purpose, I have reached a point where I believe that success is mine to be had and that I will have it. With this new realization, life has taken on a new and true meaning which has propelled me forward to begin my consulting practice and the crown jewel of my conglomerate of companies, www.MoneyByRamey.com.

Thus far, the journey has been truly astounding.

For the time being, my focus is on earning massive amounts of active income and continuing to build up my dividend portfolio through adding more shares in great companies.

Rather than take dividends as cash, I am allowing the dividends to be invested into shares and accumulate via a dividend reinvestment plan on each of my positions.

With each new fractional ownership DRIP purchase, I can see the path of Financial Freedom being laid out open before me. By taking this journey towards Financial Freedom, there is also a welcomed byproduct; the quest for personal growth.

No longer can I sit by idly, accepting a paycheck and whatever else life hands me. Since I fully know that I will soon have the Financial and Time Freedom to do what I want, when I want, I now put more emphasis on answering the burning question of "What do I want?"

To me, this has been the greatest part of this journey towards Financial Freedom. Answering the unending quest for originality in my life's purpose has become my true calling.

Unwilling to follow the prescribed dogma of what an acceptable life is, I am now out to craft a journey for myself, to lay down my own path and to discover who this awesome, crazy, human being named Matthew Ramey really is.

It is my hope that by reading this book, you can learn and grow from my triumphs as well as my mistakes. It has not all been 'rainbows and sunshine'; arduous times have set themselves before me and it is only through tenacity, grit, and divine guidance that I have found my way back home.

I also hope that in reading this you find it more than a book on dividend investment strategy. I hope that it will have you pondering on your life's meaning and purpose, and that through your journey towards Financial and Time Freedom, you will discover how to make this world a better place to live.

Humbly I say thank you for choosing to read this book. No matter who you are or where your place is in this life, you can achieve your dreams if you make it a definite goal with an actionable plan.

Welcome to our shared muse: Financial Freedom. Upward and Onward!

Simple Investing Outline

Thank you for purchasing this book! It is my sincere hope that I can teach you the basics of the dividend investing strategy, in order that you might begin implementing this wonderful investing mechanism in your own portfolio.

This book is organized into four main parts:

1. **Dividend Investing: The Basics**
2. **Dividend Investing: The Strategy**
3. **Dividend Investing: Implementation**
4. **Dividend Investing: The Strategy In Action**

Each section will build upon the last.

In **The Basics** section, you will learn my history and get introduced to what you can expect to see on the dividend investing journey.

In **The Strategy** section, you will learn the ins and outs of why dividend investing is a great form of capital allocation.

In **The Implementation** section, you will see the 'nuts and bolts' behind how the dividend investing strategy is implemented on a daily basis.

In **The Strategy In Action** section, we will analyze various stocks so that you can become familiar with the strategy and how it works in actuality.

Good luck and welcome to the journey!

Dividend Investing: The Basics

Getting Started: What You Will Need

Congratulations! By purchasing this book, you are well on your way towards the path of Financial Freedom through learning about the dividend investing strategy. Before we go any further, I'd like to further prepare you by letting you know what you'll need to continue on this path.

I learned all of this from traveling my own Financial Freedom path and want to give you the fast track in your journey towards learning more about the art of dividend investing.

#1 - A Firm Grasp of Basic Financial Concepts

In having a desire to learn more about dividend investing, you should have a firm grasp of the basic financial concepts. This means that items such as balance sheet, income statement, debt ratio, liquidity, etc. should not come as new terms.

If these do happen to be new concepts, I would recommend that you give this book a read through, write down terms that you do not understand, and then do some research on the topics as you go along.

The dividend investing journey took me many years to feel like I have finally reached some level of mastery and even now, I have so much to learn. It is only through this constant quest for knowledge that we can continually grow and propel ourselves forward.

I have personally been involved in financial analysis for the majority of my career. For about 15 years up to the point of this writing, I was involved in analyzing financials and ascertaining counterparty risk.

During this time period, I have learned much in the way of how to value companies, how to ascertain payment abilities, and perhaps most importantly, how to diagnose and spot trouble in a company's financials.

This acumen of financial analysis did not come easy though - I have read many books, blogs, articles, and watched many videos on the best investors in the world. I mercilessly studied various investment strategies and spent countless hours googling any term I did not understand. I still continue on this quest for knowledge on a daily basis. The thirst is real.

If you are not yet at the point of mastering these basic financial concepts, this is not to discourage you from beginning your journey. In fact, I would say you are on a mission to learn as much as you can, as fast as you can.

This fable told by former President John F. Kennedy summarizes the concept of when to begin:

"The great French Marshall Lyautey once asked his gardener to plant a tree. The gardener objected that the tree was slow growing and would not reach maturity for 100 years. The Marshall replied, 'In that case, there is no time to lose; plant it this afternoon!'"

You are akin to the great French Marshall. You recognize that the time to begin is right here, right now.

Start building the base for your investment strategy today. Once you have the foundation in place of mastering the basic financial concepts, then you are ready to build upon that foundation with whatever investment strategy you choose.

Spoiler Alert! I recommend a Dividend Investment Strategy!

#2 - Analytical Aptitude & Knowledge

If you desire to manage your own investment portfolio, you will want to develop an analytical tilt and the willingness to learn and understand the numbers. One of the biggest mistakes that an investor can make is 'following the herd'. This herd-type mentality has lead to financial ruin for many a Financial Freedom seeker. To understand the reason why you want to invest, you need to understand the story and the numbers behind the story.

You will need to be able to answer questions such as:

- Why would I invest my hard-earned capital into this company?

- What is this company's story?

- What are the numbers telling me?

- Where do I see this company in 10, 20, 50 years?

- Is the industry in upheaval? Or is it growing?

- Who else is investing in this company? What are the analyst's thoughts and predictions?

If you invest just because everyone else is investing in the company, I can virtually guarantee you will come to a point where that investment strategy will come back to haunt you. You may enter at too high of a valuation or find a company with growth prospects greatly overestimated by Mr. Market.

DivTalk: Mr. Market is the affectionate term for the general crazy reactions of the stock market as a whole. It is a term invested by master value investor Benjamin Graham, in his 1949 masterpiece, The Intelligent Investor.

> Mister Market is an erratic, idiosyncratic personality, which reacts to market news with quick trades that often times go against long-term reason. He is only thinking about the immediate moment, with no regard for what price he is buying or selling.

With your own analysis in place, the goal is to have your own set of reasons, regardless of what the pundits might tell you. Surely you can listen to sound advice and by all means, I recommend that you seek out as much information as realistically possible when looking to invest into a stock.

Keep in mind that at the end of the day, whether or not to invest comes down to your own personal abilities and intuition regarding the direction of the markets, and potential of the investment opportunity.

#3 - Access to the Internet

This goes without saying, but you will need a solid, reliable internet connection to buy and sell stocks. Gone are the days when you would call up your broker and ask him to buy 'x' amount of shares at 'x' amount of prices.

Now every stock trade is electronically categorized and completed; to keep up to speed with the market, you will need to learn to do the same. This brings up two compelling points with regard to current stock purchasing:

1. Most stock purchases are now very low-cost or actually fee-free.

2. You will need to buy and sell stocks when advantageous. The onus is on you to protect your money.

Markets move very fast, so being able to connect to the internet on a moment's notice is more important now than ever. Your positions are up against complicated algorithms, day traders, and massive hedge funds.

It is not realistic to ask a solo, individual investor to compete and defeat those with the dedicated resources of a multi-billion dollar hedge fund. Since I am more inclined towards being a 'buy-and-hold-forever' value investor, I am much less worried about being able to have access to buying or adding to a position at a moment's notice.

My goal is not to time the markets on initiating a position but rather to find companies at great value points for investing. However, I do recognize the fact that if Mr. Market goes erratic and provides me an excellent opportunity to invest in a stock at a level that I am comfortable with, I must be ready and willing to pull the trigger and initiate the position at a moment's notice.

More importantly, if a stock deteriorates enough in its financial value and- worst case scenario - cuts or eliminates its dividend, I need to be able to quickly ascertain the situation and look to unload my position at the highest possible price. All of this requires an active, reliable internet connection, which is why I mention this as its own separate point worth discussion.

#4 - A Willingness to Learn

You will need a willingness to be open to new knowledge and be geared towards incremental improvements in your own investing strategy. Though I have been honing my investing craft for many years, it was not until relatively recently - in the past seven years or so - that I really began to identify the investing strategy that works for me.

This journey was not an overnight revelation which, once understood, was implemented and immediately a success. Rather, it took many years of learning, much study, and much quiet contemplation before I began down the path I am currently traveling.

I started with mock portfolios, then graduated to investing small sums of money. Even now, I still adhere to position limits both on initial cash outlays and investment size. Both of these limits help me manage risk in case my analysis of a potential investment potential happens to be wrong.

DivTalk: Position limits are meant to reduce risk and protect the investor from losing more money than they can handle. I personally recommend setting position limits for yourself, especially when starting out.

When developing your strategy, you might want to start investing in $200 or $500 increments once a week. This will help limit your losses until you begin to understand and hone your own strategy. For me, I currently have a position limit of $10,000 on any one trade.

I have this self-imposed limit to 'save' myself from poor market timing and to minimize potential losses to a manageable level.

In all cases of life, but especially in stock investing, the willingness to learn is a key asset that we need to adopt and grow in order to be successful.

#5 - Patience: Wait For Values Not Timing

A friend and I had a conversation once. I was telling him about my strategy in regards to investing. He made the comment that "In investing, you cannot time the market." I agree 100% with this philosophy and he was completely accurate in his assessment.

However, there is a stark difference between timing the market and finding a good value point. As investors, we need to be on the lookout for these good valuation points when we're considering initiating a position.

This is different from timing the market in that waiting for valuations is based on analysis of the numbers and not on which way we believe the market will trend. Sometimes it may seem to be a form of timing, but value investors know that they can never predict which way the market will go. Rather, they accept that the only control they have is choosing the entry point on a new position.

It is challenging to be in the situation where they sit on the sidelines with a large amount of cash because simply because you do not feel as though valuations are where they need to be to buy into companies. Nothing is more frustrating than seeing the market rise, without your funds being actively deployed yet.

It can be tempting to want to follow the market upward and invest even though the analysis is telling us that a certain stock or industry or perhaps the market as a whole is overvalued. It is especially important that at this point, as a dividend investor focused on valuation, we must exercise patience and wait for the market to return to levels where we feel comfortable deploying our capital.

A perfect case in point of exercising this patience is the

famous investor, Warren Buffett. As of this writing, his conglomerate, Berkshire Hathaway, is sitting on a $100 billion dollar cash position (1).

Certain shareholders are requesting that he invests this money, but I can assure you that Warren Buffett will not deploy this capital unless he believes there is a good value proposition for which to use the funds.

Warren Buffett is a very patient man; in fact, he is practicing a very long-term view of patience. This means that no matter how we might feel emotionally about waiting for solid investment points, we must continue to wait until the market provides us solid entry opportunities.

As an investor, one of the things you must avoid at all costs, is loss of principal capital. This is where being patient will pay off. Even if it seems as though we are missing out on market upswings and downswings, our patience will pay dividends down the road. More on that later.

#6 - Emotional Fortitude

Investors need to have emotional fortitude in order to buy and sell companies in a logical manner. One cannot invest well into the long-term if one is ruled by emotions. It is tempting to allow ourselves to make emotional decisions when we see the numbers in our accounts going up or going down. It is only human nature.

When the numbers are going up, all is well and we are elated.

When the numbers are going down, it is a much different story.

The truth is that the investor needs to view his situation inversely from the everyday individual.

As Warren Buffett famously states:

"Be greedy when others are fearful and fearful when others are greedy."

What this means to the everyday investor is to view declines in the market as an ideal situation as it allows you to purchase stocks at better prices.

For the dividend investor in particular, this means you'll do a small "celebration dance" when the market declines - including your current positions decline in value (assuming no material financial concerns) - as this means you now get to purchase more of these wonderful stocks via reinvesting dividends. So long as the company remains in a solid position, stock declines that cause the overreaction of Mr. Market *are good for you.*

This type of emotional fortitude is not easy to come by. In my own personal journey, I have come to the point where I see that when stock prices appreciate, it can be a negative for me, as this means that stocks are becoming more expensive on the DRIP method. It is when prices are going down that I am happy as this means I will have better entry points for new positions via reinvested dividends.

#7 - Be Able to Follow the Plan

As a follower of a dividend investing strategy, it is pertinent that you are largely unattached from the day-to-day market swings. By all means, stay-tuned to the markets and your position fluctuations for material deterioration in the positions you own. However, now that you have bought an awesome company at a fair value, your main objective is to consider yourself an owner of the company.

Owners do not sell their positions at the whims of the day-to-day market; rather the owners are with the company for the long-term.

Granted, you are not involved in the company's day-to-day activities, but the main goal of a dividend investor is much the same: keep buying great companies at great prices.

To do this, your main action plan is to do the analysis and complete due diligence on any stock you are considering purchasing. Once you are satisfied that the company you are buying into is fairly valued, has market dominance, and good growth prospects, you are ready to be in a position to 'buy-and-hold' forever.

You have followed the plan; now sit back, enjoy the fruits of your hard work, and let the dividends roll in.

#8 - A Humble Confidence aka the "It" Factor

Last but not least, you must have the confidence to be a successful investor. Just as we must have confidence to be successful in any endeavor in life, dividend investing is certainly no different.

What I have found is that individuals are not just born with confidence; rather it comes through hard work, study, and putting in the hours to understand the topic at hand.

Once you have attained the proper knowledge, acumen, and are beginning to trust in your system, the next step is having the confidence in yourself to initiate positions.

In my early investing career, I found that possessing a 'humble confidence' was the most challenging part about initiating a 'buy'. I would do all the analysis and due diligence, feel certain about the growth prospects, but when it came time to buy I would hesitate. Thoughts would run through my mind:

- "What if I am wrong?"

- "What if I buy and the stock goes down?"

- "What if I buy and the stock cuts its dividend, rendering me without any stable income?"

- "What if I lose it all and become homeless as a result?"

These are not easy thoughts to counteract. Early on, these inhibited much of the potential action in purchasing solid companies at fair prices. To be fair, these thoughts relayed to me that perhaps I was not yet ready to begin investing on my own. Eventually I had to reach a point where I said, "I can do this" and simply started on my journey.

As my confidence grew, so did my position sizes. Where I once felt comfortable in investing a few hundred dollars into a position, I now am comfortable with a few thousand or tens of thousands of dollars in a new stock purchase. I do not anticipate going much higher than this for initial positions though as it increases the concentration risk in one stock, which is something I like to avoid.

One more caveat; I added the word 'humble' to confidence in a purposeful manner. Those individuals that would risk their own capital via managing their investments need to maintain a confidence that they are good at what they do yet maintain a realistic mindset that they could be wrong as well.

In having confidence without this humbleness, investors run the risk of excessive hubris which has caused the ruin of many a man and company.

So stay confident, yet stay humble. Be open to new ideas, information, and do not be afraid to admit you were wrong. I can guarantee that you will pick a wrong position at some point in time; this is normal and ok. To counteract this, ensure that the position is sized right as to not be a catastrophic loss and learn the necessary lessons to grow and improve.

Why a Dividend Investing Strategy?

The modern stock market is one of the greatest inventions in the history of humanity. By its existence, everyday individuals, no matter what their race, creed, societal standing, or stature in the world, can own the greatest companies the world over.

If you want to own a piece of Apple ($AAPL), the process is very simple: you open a brokerage account, pull up the stock ticker, input the number of shares, confirm execution price, and voila! You now own a piece of a fantastic company at a (hopefully) fantastic price point.

We routinely hear stories about the office administrator, though not a high-earner by any means, who sustained great discipline over a period of many years and decades, and as a result, retired with millions of dollars in the bank.

Though stocks will have their ups (bull market) and downs (bear market), routinely investing in publicly traded companies has represented the single greatest wealth generator over the last hundred plus years. In no other time in human history has the everyday individual been able to own shares of the largest companies the world over. This is a beautiful thing.

I personally believe that selecting companies for investment does not need to be a complex matter; the simplicity of owning great companies at great prices is the way to Financial Freedom.

When you are first starting out on your journey, the concept of early retirement through dividend investing might seem like a distant and unattainable goal. However, by implementing a dividend investment strategy, you will begin to see how that distant goal is indeed an attainable reality. How? By purchasing solid, dividend paying stocks at excellent price points.

So why dividends and not growth stocks? I will be the first to admit that I am not a great judge of a stock's growth potential. I personally believe that growth stocks can be overvalued and I am not sure what a solid entry point happens to be.

There are investors for whom the growth investment strategy is their bread and butter; to them I say 'kudos'. There is more than one way to successfully invest.

I do happen to own some investment funds that specialize in investing in growth stocks. This particular strategy where I invest in solid dividend income stocks and outsource the analysis and investment into growth stocks to others, works very well for me.

However, when it comes to investing for the long-term, dividend paying stocks on a dividend reinvestment program are a very apt combination. When these stocks are on DRIP, a runaway 'snowball' effect is created through continually rising dividends and growing positions.

A forward momentum is achieved, which if investing in the proper stocks, cannot be halted. Any growth becomes exponential, where compounding interest, commonly referred to as the eighth wonder of the world, takes its effect in the form of massive share accumulation. The results are truly amazing.

It is from this phenomenal growth that a dividend income investor can achieve the dream of becoming 'Financially Free'.

Financial Freedom: The End Goal

By investing in dividend-paying stocks, the investor makes money while he or she sleeps through dividend payments. It is only by this concept of having your money work for you that you can truly achieve Financial Freedom and, as a result, time freedom. This quote by Warren Buffet sums up this principle beautifully:

"If **you** don't find a way **to make money while you sleep**, **you** will work until **you** die."

Warren **Buffett**

I am an advocate for working hard in your day-to-day life. Whatever our hands find to do, we should do it with all of our ability and determination. By trading our hours for work, we can find a meaning and a purpose in our lives beyond just constantly being bored or entertained.

With that being said, we do want to reach a point where our money is making money for us so that we no longer need to trade our hours for work. When actively working becomes a choice and not a need, life meaning reaches a whole new level. You will then be free to pursue whatever your hobbies or purpose might be whether that is painting, spending more time with family, coaching, writing, etc. This is where a well-invested dividend portfolio comes into effect.

When you invest your hard-earned capital into dividend paying stocks, you are securing a steady income stream for the future. The idea is to have these companies pay you a routine dividend, reinvest that dividend into buying more shares of stock, and repeat until you reach a level where you are ready to turn the 'dividend cash spigot' on. Once you reach this level, the goal is to have the dividends completely cover the expenses in your life and providing some extra cash for life fun.

If your analysis proves true and the company is a good purchase at the current price with a routine dividend payment, then all you have to do is sit back and receive a consistent dividend for each share of stock that you own.

Not only will you be receiving a stable income, but if the company does well and elects to increase the dividend, you will be getting a raise as well!

The concept of living off dividend income needs only to apply to your current situation; if you are happy with having 'X' amount of dividends paid, whatever that number may be for you, then you are in a great place.

Perhaps your goal is to make enough to cover your living expenses so that you only need to work to afford food and entertainment. Perhaps you want to have dividend income cover all of your life's expenses. Whatever your case may be, with a dividend investing strategy, you're seeking to build and maintain your passive income through dividend producing stocks.

Is It Possible to Live Off Dividend Income?

Living off the income generated by dividends is not only possible but it is possible for you.

Is it a long and challenging road to get there? Yes, most definitely.

Does it take courage? You bet it takes courage, persistence, and determination.

But if you stay diligent and continue on the forward path, you can realize success!

In 2018, when I first started my MoneyByRamey.com journey, I had $566.30 in annual dividend income. I remember looking at that number, wondering how I could even get it to be at a level where it could sustain my day-to-day living expenses. After all, $500 just doesn't get you very far in this world.

However, my view was wrong. Instead of seeing $566.30 as a number set in time, I needed to see the *potential* behind that number.

The $566.30 was merely a starting point for the runaway growth that I was ready to experience. The more I invested, the quicker this number grew. Instead of being in a position of buying stocks, hoping for appreciation,and then selling my assets to pay for a retirement, I was earning *real income* and reinvesting that into accumulating more shares on a routine basis.

Through these dividend payment, I continue to grow my yearly income and hope to never have to sell a single share of the great companies that I own.

The results speak for themselves.

At the time of this publishing, my portfolio consists of 35 positions which generate $5,052.38 in annual dividend income.

The MoneyByRamey.com Dividend Portfolio

Company	Symbol	Shares	Yearly Div/share	Share Price (Today)	Annual Income	Yield	Total Value	% of Portfolio
AT&T	T	280.34	$2.04	$34.82	$571.89	5.86%	$9,761.44	7.25%
Procter & Gamble	PG	131.42	$2.98	$117.32	$392.10	2.54%	$15,418.19	11.45%
International Business Machines	IBM	49.66	$6.48	$129.57	$321.80	5.00%	$6,434.45	4.78%
West Rock	WRK	155.93	$1.82	$32.34	$283.79	5.63%	$5,042.78	3.74%
Exxon Mobil	XOM	69.46	$3.48	$67.49	$241.72	5.16%	$4,687.86	3.48%
Weyerhauser	WY	171.88	$1.36	$25.12	$233.76	5.41%	$4,317.63	3.21%
Coke	KO	135.76	$1.60	$53.74	$217.22	2.98%	$7,295.74	5.42%
Beyond Petroleum	BP	84.6	$2.46	$36.21	$208.12	6.79%	$3,063.37	2.27%
Archer-Daniels-Midland	ADM	140.75	$1.40	$37.43	$197.05	3.74%	$5,268.27	3.91%
3M Company	MMM	32.4	$5.76	$155.85	$186.62	3.70%	$5,049.54	3.75%
Pfizer	PFE	116.76	$1.44	$34.34	$168.13	4.19%	$4,009.54	2.98%
The Smuckers Company	SJM	49.12	$3.40	$111.20	$167.01	3.06%	$5,462.14	4.06%
United Postal Service	UPS	38.27	$3.84	$111.28	$146.96	3.45%	$4,258.69	3.16%
WP Carey, Inc.	WPC	35.36	$4.12	$87.73	$145.68	4.70%	$3,102.13	2.30%
Starbucks	SBUX	100.17	$1.44	$94.70	$144.24	1.52%	$9,486.10	7.04%
Tyson Foods	TSN	81.76	$1.50	$89.93	$122.64	1.67%	$7,352.68	5.46%
Kohl's Inc.	KSS	43	$2.68	$45.18	$115.24	5.93%	$1,942.74	1.44%
Cummins, Inc.	CMI	24.36	$4.56	$142.02	$111.08	3.21%	$3,459.61	2.57%
Seagate Technology	STX	41.04	$2.52	$46.92	$103.42	5.37%	$1,925.60	1.43%
Caterpillar	CAT	24	$4.12	$114.06	$98.88	3.61%	$2,737.44	2.03%

Kraft-Heinz	KHC	60.79	$1.60	$25.33	$97.26	6.32%	$1,539.81	1.14%
Goodyear Tire	GT	138.69	$0.64	$11.30	$88.76	5.66%	$1,567.20	1.16%
SpartanNash	SPTN	114.34	$0.76	$10.75	$86.90	7.07%	$1,229.16	0.91%
Anheuser-Busch InBev SA/NV	BUD	37.29	$2.03	$94.19	$75.70	2.16%	$3,512.35	2.61%
Apple, Inc.	AAPL	24.07	$3.08	$202.64	$74.14	1.52%	$4,877.54	3.62%
Delta Airlines	DAL	43.58	$1.61	$56.20	$70.16	2.86%	$2,449.20	1.82%
Fastenal	FAST	79	$0.86	$29.66	$67.94	2.90%	$2,343.14	1.74%
Ford	F	111.55	$0.60	$8.77	$66.93	6.84%	$978.29	0.73%
CenturyLink	CTL	63.66	$1.00	$11.21	$63.66	8.92%	$713.63	0.53%
Ingredion	INGR	25.19	$2.50	$75.98	$62.98	3.29%	$1,913.94	1.42%
Newell Brands	NWL	67.04	$0.92	$15.76	$61.68	5.84%	$1,056.55	0.78%
Wells Fargo	WFC	22.81	$1.80	$44.42	$41.06	4.05%	$1,013.22	0.75%
Bunge	BG	7.51	$2.00	$53.22	$15.02	3.76%	$399.68	0.30%
General Electric	GE	71	$0.04	$7.97	$2.84	0.50%	$565.87	0.42%
Cal-Maine	CALM	11.21	$0.00	$40.60	$0.00	0.00%	$455.13	0.34%

*The above portfolio is sorted by 'Annual Income'

Source: https://www.moneybyramey.com/dividend-portfolio/

The beautiful part is that once a position is initiated, the dividend portfolio is on autopilot. So long as nothing material affects operations in a negative way, these great companies will continue to pay dividends, I will continue to grow my positions, and my dividend income will continue to rise.

Case in point: I just received two dividend increases in the past month which increased my overall annual dividend income by $19.80. These increases were raises, and I had to do no additional work to receive this extra income. The

35

companies and their awesome employees continued to work hard, grow earnings, and paid me more for being an owner.

My only time investment was the initial due diligence when first considering the stock and the emotional fortitude necessary to continue holding onto the position in my portfolio.

Adopting The "Brick-By-Brick" Mentality

Seeing the potential and making daily incremental changes towards a goal is what I mean by adopting a "brick-by-brick" mentality. Often times, goals are only achieved through this mindset. Without it, I fear we are lost in a chasm of overwhelm.

In regards to my annual dividend income figure, I certainly have adopted the 'brick-by-brick' mindset.

What once began as a small number is growing month-over-month and year-over-year. The beautiful part is that I now see my current annual dividend income, not as a small number that is a long way from my end goal of $50,000 in dividend income per year, but rather $5,052.38 worth of capital that is being deployed each and every year into buying up more great stocks through electing dividend reinvestment plans.

It is the long game approach, but with each new addition to the portfolio, dividend raise and DRIP reinvestment, my portfolio is experiencing runaway growth through massive share accumulation. You can see the upward trajectory of Dividend Income: The Trend over at MoneyByRamey.com

Annual Dividend Income Tracking

Current ADI: 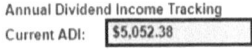 $5,052.38

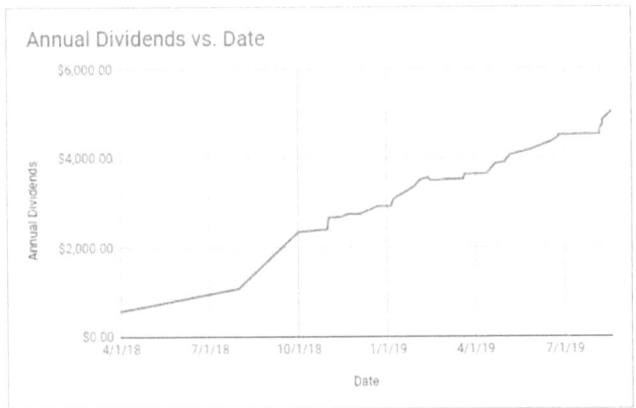

Source: https://www.moneybyramey.com/dividend-income/

What does $5,052.38 worth of annual dividend income get me? Let's see:

- If we took this annual income and averaged it out over a year, my monthly income would be $421/mo.

- More than a year's worth of tuition at my online college, Amberton University. This equals out to six MBA-level courses.

- Nearly four months of my previous $15,600 ($1300/mo.) mortgage payment.

- Fully covered annual utilities including cable, electric, and gas.

- 79% of my previous $6,374.64 ($531.22/mo.) yearly car payment.

As you can see, dividend income is real and can quickly begin to cover your life's expenses . This is important because one becomes Financially Free at the level when life's expenses can be covered by current income.

In my case, the goal is to have the dividends continue to grow to a point where they will be able to cover an entire year's worth of expenses and replace a full time income of $50,000. Once I reach that point, I will be in a position of being truly, 100% Financially Free, which is what this is all about.

For now though, these dividends are being deployed back into the awesome stocks that I own in an effort to continue growing my passive income portfolio daily!

More Reasons Why a Dividend Investing Strategy Is So Appealing

Buying and holding great dividend companies is one of the pinnacles of any investors portfolio. While I enjoy various investing strategies, I believe that a dividend investing strategy is very powerful, especially for modern day investors.

Here are some more awesome reasons to adopt a dividend investing strategy:

#1 - Passive Income Generation

Imagine this life for a second: you wake up, brew a fresh pot of coffee, and queue up a motivational video on YouTube. You are not sure what you'll be doing yet today, so you begin to figure that out. One thing you do know: your stock is going ex-dividend today and soon you will receive a nice payment of $900.

So what did you have to do to earn that income?

Well, the initial analysis and capital raise to get to the point of being able to invest was challenging and required you to trade your active hours for pay to afford the stock.

However, now that you are invested in this awesome company, all you have to do is sit back, enjoy your life, and collect the dividend payment for being an owner of a solid corporation.

This type of passive income is one of the best reasons for investing in dividend stocks.

Passive Income, simply put, is income that the investor receives without actually having to do active work to receive the income.

A stock that continues to pay dividends fits the passive income category very well. For an everyday individual, dividend investing is one of the easiest ways to reach Financial Freedom. However, even though the process of accumulating income through investing is easy, in actuality the execution is very hard.

In fact, getting to where you can live off dividends income is one of the most demanding endeavors that any investor can undertake. However, if one is able to figure out this formula and execute the process with discipline and tenacity, their future will be set for life through passive income generated through dividend payments.

#2 - Make Money While You Sleep

While you sleep, you make money. What could be more appealing than this? This is the ultimate end goal as someone seeking after Financial Freedom.

While we want to truly enjoy our work and find a sense of purpose from our everyday activities, especially from those positions that we trade our precious life hours in return for getting a paycheck, the ultimate dream is to be earning money even when not working. Owning dividend stocks serves as a vital part in assisting you in achieving this dream.

How do we make money while we sleep? By owning assets that generate passive income.

Owning stocks that pay dividends is one of the best ways I know how to generate passive income. Once you get past the initial due diligence of figuring out which companies to invest, you simply sit back and collect the dividend in routine fashion.

Once we build up a portfolio of dividend paying stocks that continue to pay us quarter-after-quarter and year-over-year, we are well on the way to having our passive income on autopilot.

Sleep soundly my friends.

#3 - Real Ownership in Companies

Let's not forget the heart of why we are investing; owning a piece of some of the greatest companies in the world. A dividend investing strategy happens to be geared toward finding companies that are well valued and pay a stable and decent dividend.

When the numbers are all said and done, we can simplify the equation of dividend investing to:

1. Ownership in great companies at fair values.

2. The company pays you a regular dividend for being an owner.

Two good questions to ask yourself when considering an ownership stake:

1. Will this company continue to operate 30, 40, 50 years from now?

2. Do I believe in the company's mission, product, and way forward?

If you can answer a definitive 'yes' to both of these questions, then you are on the right path. If the answer happens to be 'no', then you should strongly considering placing your capital elsewhere.

However, by continually investing capital into the greatest companies the world over, you are growing as these companies grow. As their employees continue working hard and growing the company revenue, you - as an owner - reap in the rewards.

#4 - Lower Tax Liability

If you are a "buy and hold forever" investor, the tax advantages of dividends are going to be your friend. I currently reside in the US, where, if you hold onto a dividend stock for more than one year, you are subjected to capital gains taxes near the 15% level or, in some cases, even less.

Considering that dividend income is very real income, yet entirely passive in nature, I welcome this low tax for being an astute manager of my money.

Let's look at this example. Say you work at a company and earn $50,000 per year. How much would you take home?:

Let's begin by assuming you are in the 25% tax bracket. Of that $50,000, you would need to pay 25% in federal tax rates.

($50,000*.25) = $12,500 owed in taxes.

Let's now say you own dividend stocks that net you $50,000 in passive income per year. How much would you take home?

($50,000*.15) = <u>$7,500 owed in taxes.</u>

As you can see, both incomes are real forms of income, but dividend income is taxed at a much lower level than regular income. In this example above, the capital gains example, you pay $5,000 less than if this were to be regular income.

Now, these are simple math calculations and do not take into account any tax advantages associated with either form of income, but the examples show just how powerful passive dividend income can truly be. This is always subject to change in the coming years and decades ahead, but for now, the advantage goes to dividend income.

#5 - Simplified Investing

In the world of investing, it can be challenging to decide which stocks to pick. Between analyst recommendations, the thousands or tens of thousands of stocks that come up on a screener search, and the everyday news of earnings, hits, misses, and everything in between, it's no wonder that investors can have trouble finding the proverbial 'needle in the hay' stock.

Selecting stocks can be a challenging proposition for any investor.

Dividend investing simplifies the selection process It allows the investor to have a solid gauge for which stocks to choose . Rather than attempt to predict the future and engage in guesswork of which direction the stock will head, the investor can ask him or herself: "What is the current dividend yield and what is the net effect to my current annual dividend income?"

By asking this question, the investor can better determine whether or not the current stock is at a solid entry point.

Rather than an arbitrary percentage being given as the metric for investment success or failure, the dividend investor can point to their dividend income as positive proof of the solidness of their investing strategy.

Which brings me to my next point.

#6 - Motivation By Being Focused on ADI

Investors who follow a dividend investing strategy can rest assured that their motivation will stay high by following the trend of their annual dividend income (ADI) rather than the erratic market swings.

In deploying our hard earned capital into stocks, only one thing is certain: markets will fluctuate, both positively and negatively.

As investors, it feels good to see our stocks gaining value. Anything in the green is welcomed news.

However, our positions will be down from time-to-time, in which case emotions can easily take over and we see paper losses as actual losses. It is during these time periods that ADI can help smooth things over.

By focusing in on annual dividend income, we can let the everyday market swings go right on by while we continue to see our ADI going up. It will be through this focus on ADI, which is gained by reinvesting our shares through a DRIP strategy, that we can truly attain the 'set-it-and-forget-it' mode of investing.

#7 - The "Snowball Effect" through DRIP

I personally believe that DRIP investing is one of the greatest benefits to modern day investors. We'll go into this concept in more detail, but the fact that we can continually have our positions pay us dividends, and then reinvest those dividends back into the stocks that we own is such a blessing.

Not only do we continue to get income from our company's solid operations, but we have to do little work to continue growing our ownership stakes. Unless you decide to take the dividends as cash, I recommend to continue growing your position in dividend paying stocks via DRIP and let the snowball effect achieve runaway growth all on its own.

The MoneyByRamey.Com Story

Before we get into the heart of the dividend investing strategy, I would like to tell you a little bit of how I began in the world of investing my own capital.

The Dream: Financial Freedom

I have always been a curious individual. Ever since I started researching potential careers, I found that the study of high-level strategy appealed to me.

The vision of seeing myself in a boardroom, directing a team of individuals towards objectives and goals which were bigger than myself really got my juices flowing. There was no doubt in my mind as to what I would become; a very successful businessman. I would build up several conglomerates and live a cushy life in early retirement.

This dream has changed since my early days. After having various experiences in the working world, I realized that climbing the corporate ladder is not my idea of success.

Being relegated to playing politics, dressing in a suit and tie everyday, and speaking in corporate jargon is no longer as appealing to me. It is not that the idea of becoming a CEO has changed, rather the vision and what it would mean to lead has morphed and developed over the years.

This has lead to a reorganization of my priorities. If I do not want to work in a large company and work my way to the top, then what do I want to do? I found that my heart and soul is geared towards working with SMEs (Small-Mid Sized Enterprises) in an entrepreneurial capacity. There is something so invigorating from getting into a start-up or small operation from the ground floor and helping to develop and build its operations.

I realized there were two main reasons why I enjoyed working with these smaller entities:

1. I get to wear many different hats which keeps my mind constantly engaged,

2. There is a higher chance that I get to do what I want, when I want.

From this vantage point, I began the search for a lifestyle that fit this mindset. I knew that to be successful in this arena, I had to arrive at a point where I was making enough money to cover my daily expenses while making enough profit to ensure a comfortable lifestyle.

I knew that I could build businesses based on systems, but I also knew that I wanted more. I wanted to be Financially Free so that I would never have to depend on only one income stream to support my career. After all, isn't relying on only one company via salary a riskier proposition than developing multiple income sources?

In my mind, I wanted the multiple income sources offered through entrepreneurship. More than this, I became enamored with the idea of becoming Financially Free and living off of passive income.

Now that I had the dream, I had to answer the question: how do I earn more passive income and achieve Financial Freedom?

How I Can Earn Passive Income?

Enter the world of passive income. I am a finance major by trade but I will admit that it took me a while before I really took the idea of passive income generation seriously.

Growing up, I learned the concept of the time value of money, accumulating interest income, and a general sense of how to invest. However, even though I mastered these concepts, I never really gained a concept of what it would mean to have my money working for me.

It seemed that everyone around me was so busy making ends meet that they did not seem to have time for anything else. Constantly rising needs and wants meant that the active income had to keep flowing in uninterrupted. If the main source of money was dried up, then it would send them into panic mode. If one block was removed from the pyramid, everything would fall.

There is some merit to living this way. An apt quote that comes to mind:

"Do you want to take the island? Then burn the boats."

-Julius Caesar

This seems to be a quote that many are destined to live by. For when lifestyle needs increase and thus the corresponding debt levels rise in unison, survival instincts kick into high gear and one seeks after more and more ways to make higher income to cover the expenses.

However, I saw this way of living as fleeting. I did not want to be caught up in the game of ever increasing wants and an ever increasing means to keep my head above the 'rising tide' of expenditures and debt accumulation.

Rather, I began to see how passive income could become my way to having my life expenses paid for by the passive income streams which I had developed.

How Did I Start?

I enjoy hard work, but I loathe being tied down to a position. I know that some people enjoy the stability and security of a full-time job. To me though, being regulated to a schedule and a day-to-day routine is a version of death. There is just something suffocating about being in a position where if I wanted to leave, I would be risking too much.

It may sound extreme, but it is my reality.

I first noticed this in high school, although I wasn't consciously aware of it at the time. I was a decent student, earning B/C grades and mostly staying out of trouble. However, the routine monotony of the daily school schedule wore me down. I did not thrive.

School is designed to educate and prepare students for the working world; arrive at a certain time, lunch break, then end at a certain time. These are mechanisms geared toward conditioning students for the 9-5pm work environment.

The powers that be sure start us out young.

In general, I have no qualms about this system. I feel like the majority of the population fit in well into this system of operation.

Most people desire a full-time position, a company with benefits, and the same routine of the day-to-day environment. But for creative types like me, it is challenging, if not impossible to work in this kind of environment.

Environments where I develop most have the unifying theme of constant change through welcomed challenge.

Enter the College Years

In college, I found my niche. Being able to set my own schedule and be responsible for the results, invigorated and lead me to such success that I ended up graduating Cum Laude with a 3.81 GPA and Outstanding Graduate for Management Major.

I don't mean to brag; I only wish to demonstrate that in these years, I found that with positions in which I was responsible for results and the mechanisms toward attainment, the outcome was high levels of success. I learned that I am most prosperous in a loose structure with room for creative outlet.

Looking back, I also see that I am at my best when working on projects with a specific completion objective and a specific end date in mind. This is an interesting observation which I have only recently begun to really understand its impact.

I am much more of a builder and designer as opposed to someone geared towards a 'maintenance mode' mentality.

I believe that this mindset helps me in my quest for a dividend portfolio that generates $50,000 in annual dividend income. Instead of seeing this as a monstrous goal that cannot be achieved, I utilize the 'brick-by-brick' mindset and begin to see the small, incremental steps I am making towards this goal.

With each new purchase, my motivation level is reinvigorated and it is almost as though the journey begins anew. I really started to connect with this when being engaged in financial topics.

Finance Beckons

The world of finance began to loom large. I found that numbers appealed to me, and thus I began on a path of trying to understand everything there was to know about investing. I began to read articles on Buffett and followed the market trends on a daily basis.

I still had no idea what many of the terms that I was reading meant, but I had the thirst and desire to learn more.

This was also the period in my life where I began to manage my own money, albeit in a smaller capacity than I currently do.

In my first book, *Simple Budgeting*, I detailed how I began a world-class budgeting process after my checking account was assessed a late fee. It was then that I discovered that I absolutely hated unnecessary expenses. As a result of this experience, I vowed that I would become a master of finances so I would never lose out on my money again via an unnecessary expense.

I began an internship in the world of private equity, where I was part of the new business development team. I was only 21, yet was charged with targeting industries ripe with investment potential.

The routine was simple; you find a target industry ready for consolidation via a stock screener analysis, attain and prepare a mailing list, and then follow up with endless calls with upper-level management. The goal was to talk to the decision-makers - CFOs, CEOs, business owners.

The job was certainly interesting and the takeaways were many. However, my biggest lesson learned with this job was the necessity of balance in my life. In this internship, the expectations were that you arrive early and stay late. By "arrive early", I meant that we were expected to be there at 7am and leave no earlier than 9pm. If you didn't put in 12+ hour workdays, you were a slacker.

While I enjoy making money and working hard, I quickly learned that the idea, "making money is all there is in life" did not appeal to me. Seeing the partners - owners capable of making millions of dollars per year - sacrificing their families, hearts, and souls in the process, turned me off to the idea that such a life was for me.

In fact, it taught me more about what I didn't want and in the end, this lesson helped me focus even more on what I truly did want.

So What Else Is There?

If I didn't want to work myself to exhaustion, then what else was there? I loved to write and teach the game of basketball, but at the time I didn't see how to turn either of those ideas into full-time earning potential. Instead, I decided to move back to MN and enter into the corporate working world.

It was an interesting experience. Being in the corporate environment was much like being back in high school. You have a set time for arriving to work, you get a lunch break, and then you work until the day is over.

Many people enjoy this security and structure; however, being someone that thrives on change and unconventionality, I soon found this type of environment suffocating. I also found it abhorrent that someone else was controlling my time.

Even though I learned much from the experience of being in the corporate world, I began to feel that something was missing from my life. I was a cog in a massive wheel that would continue to function even if I wasn't there tomorrow.

There is something reassuring about that concept but also sad; what difference was I making on a day-to-day basis? I felt small and it was hard to match up my daily contributions to the betterment of society.

I began the quest for understanding how to break free of the system. Around this time I began to dive into the world of investing on my own. With a general fury and focus, I took on the task of gaining an even deeper understanding of the investment world; terms, definitions, and how to analyze financial statements - nothing was off-limits.

It helped that a large part of my job was financial analysis, so it all seemed to flow together.

One day, I decided to take the plunge. I bought two companies; one in the mortgage sector (because I grew up with real estate) and one in the energy sector (because the employer I worked for was invested in those companies). I bought smaller positions in both; $2,000 and $500, respectively.

The results were not what I expected.

I lost everything. Both companies headed for bankruptcy within two years. This was around 2008 when the sub-prime mortgage crisis hit home and hit hard, which caused the mortgage company to undergo unsustainable write-downs. The energy company was took large losses when the general crisis caused oil prices to tank, sending the company into unprofitable territory.

As an investor, it was a tough shake out. It would take me some years to recover emotionally from these losses. Questions were planted in my mind: do I even know how to invest? Should I just leave this to a professional? Perhaps investing isn't my forte.

However, the still small voice told me: I wasn't yet ready to invest on my own and I needed to learn much more to be a successful investor. The dream was not dead, only delayed.

A Book and A Blog: Value Investing and Dividends

After a little bit of time to recover from my losses, I was back to learning mode. I failed and needed to discover why. To be gentle on myself, it was the heart of the sub-prime crisis which many investors did not see coming and performed equally as bad, if not worse.

Instead of sulking in my losses, I realized I needed to learn more. I began exploring more about the world of investing. I read the Investors Business Daily and The Wall Street Journal to find something that would fit.

Eventually, I stumbled upon a book and a blog that would help me solidify my investing strategy.

The Book: The Intelligent Investor

The book that I discovered was Ben Graham's The Intelligent Investor. Being that I wanted to learn from the best, I had been reading and listening to Warren Buffett quite frequently. He mentioned over and over the name Ben Graham as one of his investment gurus. I decided to explore for myself.

What I discovered was a whole new way to view investing in stocks. Graham wrote of finding stocks that had deeply discounted intrinsic value relative to its current market value and then investing capital into those companies.

He displayed example after example of companies that he bought at prices which valued the stock at less than the amount of cash and working capital on hand. Keep in mind that he did much investing during the downturn of the Great Depression, so deals were easy to come by.

Regardless, I was amazed.

Could stock investing really be this easy?

Could it simply be seeing companies as ownership and buying positions?

Certainly there is more that goes into investing than this, but the principle remains the same; stock is ownership in the companies you know and trust.

With new motivation in hand, I continued to seek out more and more knowledge as my investing strategy began to take root. I stumbled upon a blog that would change my view on investing forever.

The Blog: The Dividend Mantra

The blog that I came across no longer exists in its original intent, but it was equally important in guiding my own investment process. The former author, Jason Fieber, maintains his lifestyle while now living in Thailand on the dividend income he receives from his 'Freedom Fund'.

After reading his blog, I was hooked. It was amazing reading his journey towards being financially independent. He also had a twist of minimalism in his blog, which helped to form my foray into the world of needing and wanting less.

Slowly it became apparent to me; if he can do it, so can I. I used his blog as inspiration for my own journey. I wasn't quite ready yet to completely begin my journey, but the fire was growing.

The Dividend Investing Strategy Forms

From these two sources, the high-level takeaways were:

1. Owning a stock is actually owning a piece of a company.

2. Receiving dividends is a real form of income generation.

Fast forward 10-ish years ahead, and here I sit, writing this, with a $134k portfolio that generations $5k+ in annual dividend income. While I am a long way from my end goal of $50k of annual dividend income per year, I have seen my portfolio grow roughly 446% in the past year on a combination of new purchases, DRIP, and general dividend increases.

I am here, sharing my dividend story, in order to help motivate, inspire, and guide those seeking the path of Financial Freedom.

I have seen how it can work for me and I know it can work for you too. The path is certainly not easy and requires many hours of study, hard work, and focus, but it is possible if you want to walk it.

So without further delay, it is time to jump from the general introduction of Simple Investing to the actual strategy behind dividend investing.

The Dividend Investing Strategy

So you are ready to invest on your own and want to learn more about the strategy behind dividend investing.

Well, you have come to the right place.

By utilizing a dividend investing strategy, I am confident that you are on the path to Financial Freedom via buying great companies at great prices. I have personally executed this strategy with my own funds and the results have been outstanding.

I firmly believe that this strategy, when executed properly, can and will yield outstanding results in your financial life. Learning and executing it requires a patient mindset backed with emotional fortitude that will see you through the inevitable fluctuations caused by Mr. Market.

You will see ups, and you will see downs, but so long as you are well diversified and hedged properly, this will not cause a material decline in your portfolio.

In fact, you will begin to see market declines as welcome buying opportunities, and in doing so, begin to own more and more of the companies whose products and services you use on a daily basis. Through purchasing great companies at lower prices and increasing your current positions through DRIP investing, you will be executing and living the dividend lifestyle.

Before we go any further, let's dive into an overview of the Dividend Investing Strategy.

Dividend Investing Strategy: An Overview

The dividend investing strategy is one that complements value investors well. It all begins by identifying companies that are adequately valued and also pay a good, stable dividend.

By investing in the most iconic brands the world over and maintaining those positions on a Dividend Reinvestment Plan (DRIP), you are building your way to wealth and the ultimate goal: Financial Freedom through passive income.

In becoming a dividend investor, we are committing ourselves to viewing stock ownership a bit differently. We tend to take the long-term view on the positions we own.

So what concepts make up a Dividend Investing Strategy?

"Buy-and-Hold Forever" Investing

As an investor keen on deploying capital into companies that are well-valued, my temperament is geared towards an ownership mentality in those companies I choose to invest in.

I am inclined to a 'Buy-and-Hold forever' strategy as opposed to someone who is out to day trade towards millions. Each stock that I own is not just a byte or bit to trade for short-term holding, but rather proof that I have a valid ownership stake in the company and its ongoing operations.

Investing in dividend stocks is oftentimes viewed as 'unsexy' by the market as a whole. It is written off as a strategy reserved for the sincerely risk-averse, old grandmas, and novice investors.

However, I have been executing this strategy for quite some

time and I am more than pleased with the results. Not only do I get a chance at ownership, but I also get paid regularly as well.

It's a win-win situation in my mind.

Of particular interest to me is the long-term view that a dividend investor needs to adopt in order to successfully execute this blueprint: viewing stocks as radical ownership.

I Am An Owner: The Company's Success is My Success

If the company succeeds, I succeed.

If the company grows its operations, then I grow along with it.

It is such an easy concept that connects me to the companies that I invest in, I wonder why some individuals make investing more complicated than it needs to be.

Through buying in at solid entry points and owning through the ups and downs, I continue to see my positions grow.

There are three main paths in which my investment portfolio increases:

1. **Stock Appreciation**: These are gains that come by the market valuing the stock higher, continuing to buy common shares, thus driving up the price. It is a classic supply and demand in action.

2. **Dividend Increases**: These are gains that come by the companies increasing their dividend payments, either through a percentage increase of the actual dividend or by increasing the frequency at which the dividend is paid.

3. **Share Accumulation through DRIP**: These are gains that come from continuing to buy more and more of the companies that I own through DRIP.

It is my sincere hope that I will never have to sell a position in my portfolio. The dividend investing strategy is based around the idea of buying and holding solid companies that continue to pay good dividends.

Now, will it ring true that I will never have to sell a stock due to dividend decreases or poor performance? I am not naive enough to believe so.

Just like any other investor, some of my stocks will perform well, some will perform poorly, but so long as my due diligence happens to remain on point, the positions that outperform will outweigh the positions that do not.

The point is: I choose to be an owner in the companies in which I deploy my hard-earned capital. Each time I buy a product that the company makes or see someone else purchasing a name brand I hold in my portfolio, I smile to myself because my company is succeeding and I am getting paid.

For example, my portfolio currently consists of many products I use on a daily basis:

- Starbucks ($SBUX) - Supporting my daily dose of morning happiness.

- Coke ($KO) - I enjoy a nice Diet Coke or Coke from time-to-time.

- Delta ($DAL) - I might not fly daily, but whenever I do fly, I typically fly Delta. It feels good to know that I'm supporting a stock that I own.

- AT&T ($T) - My wireless provider.

- Procter & Gamble ($PG) - a company that I use for many daily products: Tide detergent, Dawn dishwashing soap, Crest toothpaste, etc.

The list continues to grow as I add more companies to the MoneyByRamey.com portfolio.

Each time that I make a purchase from a company in which I own stock, I have a sense of pride that I am supporting a business in which I am an owner. I also take a moment to look around and see many others supporting these same businesses. This ability to tie in stock ownership to real-world applicability helps me to know that I am on the right path forward.

Another beautiful thing about the dividend investing strategy is that I'm not in some target-date fund with little cognizance of what stocks are currently being held. Rather, I am buying up companies that are well-valued and whose products I am utilizing on a daily basis.

This type of ownership-thinking helps me to stay emotionally detached in the upcoming large market swings, especially downswings. Keep in mind that I said 'upcoming' on purpose.

This is because there is only one main truth in the world of investing: the market will go up, and the market will go down.

No matter which direction the market moves, this one constant holds true no matter what your investing strategy: Mr. Market is erratic.

Mr. Market is Erratic

When asked what the market would do on a particular day, world-class investor JP Morgan famously replied,

"It will fluctuate."

Mr. Market, the endearing term for the oftentimes crazy market swings, is certainly a character.

He sometimes is so happy that he buys every stock available, no matter what the value or price.

And there are other times where he thinks the world will end tomorrow, so he sells out of nearly all of his positions as quickly as possible, even though it means selling out his ownership stake in some of the most valuable companies in the world.

Being that Mr. Market can be so erratic, I have found that measuring my own personal performance by the absolute metric of gain or loss is a losing proposition. Why?

Take this example: I have a great entry buy point on a stock, but the market, overvaluing the gloom and doom scenario, sends this perfectly good company's stock price spiraling downward. I now have a "loss".

Do I sell out now because the stock has gone down in price? Or do I choose to see that the stock is now trading at an even better valuation metric? In most cases, I'll choose the latter line of thinking.

It is when Mr. Market gives us an opportunity that we must take advantage. Enter the concept of valuing stocks based on dividends.

Dividends Are Stable, Percentages are Not

As a long-term value investor, I choose not to measure my success by a percentage gain or loss on an investment. To do so is to directly oppose the mentality of ownership after which we seek.

Remember, we want to view each share of stock as if we have absolute ownership in each company we invest in.

Buffett is fond of saying that as investors, we should be comfortable owning a stock even if the markets will be shut down tomorrow with no set date for reopening.

Is this how you view stock ownership?

For me, I currently have my screener set to view stocks by two main metrics:

1. Dividend yield

2. Valuation points

Everything else being equal, the better entry point I see on these two metrics, the more firm I am on my purchase price.

Why do I believe this is the way to invest? Simply put, I cannot time the markets.

While I believe I can pick good entry points through seeing solid valuations, there will be times that I make a great investment in a company, yet my timing will be off, so my percentage yield will be negative.

I choose to see that even in the above situation, I have made a good investment even if I currently have a "loss" on the books. This is because I can buy more of the company than before through DRIP. More on that later.

Now, just to be clear, we do want capital appreciation on our positions. These type of gains shows that the companies we are investing in are growing in value, specifically in the eyes of the general market.

However, to view a percentage gain as the only valuable metric after which we seek plays directly into the idea of 'herd mentality' investing. As diligent investors, this is the type of group-think of which we need to divorce ourselves.

Think Different

Choose to think differently than the herd. What exactly is 'herd mentality' investing?

Buying because everyone else is buying or selling because it is what the market is doing.

In other words, "Following the Herd" regardless of what market data is telling you. This is an unwise way to invest, especially if we are value investors.

Instead, our goal is to invest against the general sentiment. We want to buy when others are selling and sell when others are buying. To do so, we need to remain disciplined and unemotional in the face of large market swings.

Warren Buffet sums up exactly what we need to believe as investors:

"Be fearful when others are greedy and greedy when others are fearful."

This mindset is easier said than done. I will be one of the first to admit that I like seeing when my stocks are in the green (gains) and hate to see stocks in the red (losses).

Though this is certainly my gut instinct, I must be conscious of its fallacy: it views stocks merely as blips and numbers that go up and down. Instead, I must fight that logic and see each share that I own as absolute ownership in a great company.

So if we are more concerned with ownership, less concerned about percentage gain or loss, then what do we need to utilize as our investing metric?

Enter the concept of annual dividend income.

It's All About the Annual Dividend Income

One principle that makes a dividend investment strategy ideal is that the investor has one high-level metric to gauge progress: annual dividend income (ADI).

By keeping the high-level ADI metric in mind, the investor can make better guided, longer-term investment decisions.

Is the stock market as a whole dropping yet annual dividend income remains the same or grows through Dividend Reinvestment Plans and dividend increases? Then all is well.

With a dividend investing strategy, whether the markets drop significantly or rise exponentially becomes less important so long as the dividend remains intact and the underlying fundamentals of the stock are in place.

In fact, dividend investors welcome market downturns more than average investors because it is a chance to buy solid companies at "fire-sale" prices. In addition to making purchases in the open market at lower entry points, dividend investors also accumulate more shares via dividend reinvestment programs (DRIP).

Before we go any further, let's quickly look into the concept of DRIP.

What is DRIP?

DRIP is an acronym that stands for a Dividend Reinvestment Plan. Any brokerage firm worth their salt will be able to have your investments on an automatic reinvestment option.

For the typical small investor, having stocks on this DRIP system where dividends are automatically reinvested back into your positions, is one of the best things to ever happen in modern-day investing.

The concept of DRIP is similar to that of dollar-cost averaging. Dollar-cost averaging is the idea that investors keep buying a set amount of securities at regular intervals, regardless of market prices. Thus by engaging in these purchases on a routine basis, investors take the timing equation out of the markets, and eventually an 'average' is achieved during both market highs and lows.

The benefit to the investor is they have been routinely adding to their stock portfolios in an attempt to 'average out' their purchase prices.

When buying a stock that pays a dividend that is on DRIP, each time that you get paid a dividend, that money will automatically purchase you more shares of that stock. The great thing for any investor is that your investing strategy is on a "set-it-and-forget-it" mode.

You will only be charged with doing the initial due diligence and maintaining some cognizance of where the stock is currently at and where its directionality is trending.

Take the following example:

- You buy $2,000 worth of shares of AT&T (T) at $30.00.

- This will net you 66.7 shares of the stock.

- Assuming a quarterly dividend payment of $0.51, you will receive an annual dividend income per share of $2.04.

- Spread out across 66.7 shares, you will receive $136 in dividend income per year.

- With this $136 in annual dividend income, you will be purchasing roughly 4.53 additional shares of $T per year through DRIP investing, assuming the stock price of $30 remains relatively intact.

● Thus by the end of the year, you will have 71.23 shares of T, which will represent an increase in your position, which will increase the amount of dividends you receive (aka the snowball effect).

Here is the AT&T Forward Dividend Calculator excerpt:

Forward Dividend Calculator

Investment Amount	$2,000.00
Stock Ticker	T
Company	AT&T
Share Price	$30.00
Dividend	$0.51
Dividend Frequency	4
Annual Dividend Payout	$2.04
Shares Purchased	66.7
Payout/Yr.	$136.00
Payout/Qtr.	$34.00
Yield	6.80%
Share Accumulation	4.53

Source: https://www.moneybyramey.com/dividend-income-calculator/

I personally find that having stocks on DRIP works really well for me, because it takes out the additional research needed to initiate a new position. Often times the initial deep-diving due diligence into a company is the most challenging endeavors in buying a stock.

Not only do you need to compute and review financials, but

you also need to understand the company, its story, its products and so much more about the company and its operations. Many questions need to be asked and answered:

- What investment do I want to look into?
- Is now a good time to invest in this company?
- Is this company adequately valued?
- What is the company's current trajectory in both its industry and earning power?
- Who else is currently investing in this company?
- What does the company do and is it sustainable in a technologically advancing world?

While the initial due diligence can be difficult, finding these companies in the first place can be a 'needle in the haystack' proposition. You start with hundreds, if not thousands of companies to choose from. The goal then is to pick the current top dividend paying companies to invest in which are at reasonable valuation levels.

The difficult part is that this 'top list' can change year-over-year, month-over-month, even day-over-day. It is unrealistic to ask an investor to manage and understand such large amounts of changes with such short time spans.

Instead, when you have a stock that is automatically being repurchased for you which you have identified as being at a good value point, the additional legwork is taken out of the equation. You keep buying great companies at current market prices.

By having our stock purchases on autopilot through a dividend reinvestment plan, we are well on our way to financial freedom through quick share accumulation.

ADI + DRIP = Quick Share Accumulation

Quick share accumulation is where the beauty of dividend investing really comes into play. By having our positions on DRIP and continually using our dividends to buy more and more shares, we are steadily and consistently increasing our ownership positions. Even if our efforts result in buying only fractional ownership, we are increasing our stake nonetheless.

The results?

More Shares = More Dividends.

More Dividends = More Passive Income.

More Passive Income = More Financial Freedom.

More Financial Freedom = More Time Freedom.

Time Freedom = What this journey is all about.

What a beautiful thing.

To illustrate this, I will use a metaphor. There is a concept in dividend investing referred to as "The Snowball Effect".

The SnowBall Effect

For those of you in Minnesota or other locations with snowy climates, when I state 'building a snowball or snowman', you will know what I mean. For the rest of you, stay with me as I illustrate.

When you begin to roll up snow into a snowball, you start very small, most likely with a ball in your hands no bigger than a tennis ball.

By rolling the small snowball along the ground, it accumulates more and more snow. As you roll it, it gets bigger and bigger, and the volume increases even more due to runaway growth.

If you so desire, it will eventually get to a point where you will have increased the original size of the ball by one thousandfold! And voila, the beginning of a snowman is born!

The small snowball sure starts off small but experiences exponential growth very quickly.

Stocks on DRIP are much the same. While you might start out with a small dividend income position, if you can stay the course and continue to reinvest in your positions, you will see the same runaway growth!

The SnowBall Effect In Action: Ford

Let's look at an example: Ford ($F). The stock has been beaten up on news of Chinese tariffs and is currently trading around $9.00 with a quarterly dividend payment of $0.15 cents. At a $1,000 entry point, the annual payout would be $68.42. Here is the breakout:

Forward Dividend Calculator

Investment Amount	$1,000.00
Stock Ticker	F
Company	Ford
Share Price	$8.77
Dividend	$0.15
Dividend Frequency	4
Annual Dividend Payout	$0.60
Shares Purchased	114.0
Payout/Yr.	$68.42
Payout/Qtr.	$17.10
Yield	6.84%
Share Accumulation	7.80

If this position is on DRIP, each time a dividend is paid, you will accumulate more and more shares. Assuming things stayed constant from year-to-year (price point, dividend, etc.), here are the numbers for incremental DRIP increases:

Power of DRIP

93.82%

	Divs Received	# of New Shares Purchased	# of Shares Owned	Portfolio Value	Annual Dividend Income	Additional Investment
Year 0	$0.00	0.00	114.03	$1,000.00	$68.42	$0.00
Year 1	$68.42	7.80	121.83	$1,068.42	$73.10	$0.00
Year 2	$73.10	8.33	130.16	$1,141.51	$78.10	$0.00
Year 3	$78.10	8.90	139.07	$1,219.61	$83.44	$0.00
Year 4	$83.44	9.51	148.58	$1,303.05	$89.15	$0.00
Year 5	$89.15	10.17	158.75	$1,392.19	$95.25	$0.00
Year 6	$95.25	10.86	169.61	$1,487.44	$101.76	$0.00
Year 7	$101.76	11.60	181.21	$1,589.21	$108.73	$0.00
Year 8	$108.73	12.40	193.61	$1,697.93	$116.16	$0.00
Year 9	$116.16	13.25	206.85	$1,814.09	$124.11	$0.00
Year 10	$124.11	14.15	221.00	$1,938.21	$132.60	$0.00

Over a 10 year period, with dividends reinvested, you would nearly double your original investment and annual dividend income. Not bad right?

Well what if you invested an additional $1,000 in years 2-7? Here is the same DRIP scenario with an additional $1,000 invested over the course of 5 years:

Power of DRIP

148.65%

	Divs Received	# of New Shares Purchased	# of Shares Owned	Portfolio Value	Annual Dividend Income	Additional Investment
Year 0	$0.00	0.00	114.03	$1,000.00	$68.42	$0.00
Year 1	$68.42	121.83	235.85	$2,068.42	$141.51	$1,000.00
Year 2	$141.51	130.16	366.01	$3,209.93	$219.61	$1,000.00
Year 3	$219.61	139.07	505.08	$4,429.53	$303.05	$1,000.00
Year 4	$303.05	148.58	653.66	$5,732.58	$392.19	$1,000.00
Year 5	$392.19	158.75	812.40	$7,124.77	$487.44	$1,000.00
Year 6	$487.44	55.58	867.98	$7,612.22	$520.79	$0.00
Year 7	$520.79	59.38	927.37	$8,133.01	$556.42	$0.00
Year 8	$556.42	63.45	990.81	$8,689.43	$594.49	$0.00
Year 9	$594.49	67.79	1,058.60	$9,283.91	$635.16	$0.00
Year 10	$635.16	72.42	1,131.02	$9,919.07	$678.61	$0.00

*Keep in mind that this DRIP model and the Forward Dividend Income Calculator are only tools. It is used to help us predict dividends and contemplate potential scenarios, not provide exact data.

The percentage goes from 93.82% to 148.65% and dividend income increases 10x the original dividend income amount!

We are certainly making a lot of assumptions here since a myriad of factors could change. The company could quit paying dividends, the stock price could spiral up or down, or the company could be bought out in an acquisition or declare bankruptcy over challenging economic conditions.

However, if the dividend stays intact, share accumulation through DRIP is truly astounding. Keep in mind that this annual dividend income is passive income; the exact type of income stream that allows us to achieve the financial and time freedom we desire in our lives.

There is nothing the investor needs to do to keep earning this income other than to stay invested. The only real 'job' of the dividend investor is to monitor the positions in the portfolio from time-to-time and make sure no material deterioration has occurred.

Dividend Investing Is Simple But Not Easy

Implementing a dividend investing strategy is simple but not easy. I do believe it is well worth the time and effort it takes to learn it.

When done correctly, you can build your way to a nice, steady income stream through quarterly dividend payments. All it takes to begin is a small amount of capital, a willingness to learn, and a tenacious spirit to persevere.

Let's move onto 5 keys to remember in our dividend investing strategy.

Dividend Investing Strategy: 5 Keys to Remember

Key #1 You Are An Owner

It is the goal of an astute investor to see investments in companies as actual ownership. In this day and age, there is a trend to see stocks as simply numbers that go up and down. While that is true in some respects, let's never forget what those numbers actually mean; ownership of some in the best companies the world over.

When you are investing, make sure to keep in mind that you are not just buying stock - you, in fact, are becoming an owner in a company. Sure, for most of us, we are 'small-time' owners, but owners nonetheless. As soon as you grasp that you are taking ownership in companies rather than buying and selling an electronic number, your whole investment strategy will go to a new level.

Key #2 Income is King

In regards to investing, I am primarily concerned about one number: dividend income. Whether or not a stock goes up or down in value is of little consequence to me so long as the fundamental strength remains. I find that this type of metric keeps me locked onto the main goal of generating income.

I also find that maintaining focus on the income metric keeps me focused on the end goal: a dividend portfolio that kicks of dividend income that can support me through ups and downs in the market. This type of focus helps to divorce me from the natural rises and falls that is so inherent to everyday markets.

Key #3 The Dividend Payment is All There Is

In all portfolios, stocks will go up and down, which is completely normal. We are only concerned about two things : is the dividend stable or increasing, and will the payout continue to be covered in the years to come?

So long as the dividend is covered, we are fine with any market fluctuations that will occur. The only thing that cannot happen is the dividend being cut or eliminated altogether. That is an immediate condition for re-review and probable selling of the stock.

DivTalk: One area of concern here is that if we sell the stock when the dividend is cut or eliminated, then we are most likely selling at a low point in the stock's market price. Being value investors, this goes directly against two of our principles: 1) Buy Low, Sell High, 2) Hold for the long-term.

In making a decision to sell, we need to be extra diligent and make sure that it is because the stock is no longer appealing to use as dividend income investors and that the future does not look bright. If that is the case, then selling might be the right move.

Case in point: I bought a position in Cal-Maine (CALM) a few years ago. It has an excellent balance sheet and is involved in the food sector, which is where I wanted to keep deploying capital. I've learned that the stock only issues a dividend when it has been profitable. This means the dividend is cut during tough times. Since this company has a great balance sheet, I continue to hold this position, even though the dividend is cut from time-to-time.

We will delve more into this aspect in our chapter on the strategy in action, but it bears repeating; this goal is to invest in companies that can maintain and grow its dividend.

By doing so, you are ensuring that the companies you are investing in will continue to be here for the long haul as they have shown the ability to continue building and growing operational income.

Key #4 Diversification is Your Friend

Will all my stocks continue down the path of growth and a solid dividend payment? I surely hope so, however, I am cognizant of the dynamics of market changes and the unpredictability of all investments. Therefore diversification across various stocks and sectors is key to a good investment strategy.

If one stock is down, another is usually up, which counteracts the emotional turmoil from seeing your positions in the red rather than in the green.

I continue to hold the view that a well-diversified portfolio helps to not only reduce emotional turmoil but also reduces risk through spreading capital within various companies, sectors, etc.. My current goal is that I will limit the largest position in my portfolio to 15% of my overall holdings. By having this percentage matrix, it helps de-risk my portfolio.

DivTalk: Limiting the percentage in any one investment is known as implementing a 'position limit'. Position limits can fluctuate as market changes take place. These limits can also become skewed with large swings in our portfolios. If a position gets out of balance compared with the rest of the portfolio, it might be time to sell or buy to re-balance.

If one stock trims its dividend, or worst case, bites the bullet, I have many other stocks that will still be performing reasonably well. This 15% may grow or change as I reanalyze the risks inherent in my portfolio but for now, it serves as a great level to cap my overall risk exposure to one particular investment.

Key #5 You Are In This For The Long-Haul

Since you are geared toward value plays and dividend income, you can remove yourself from the erratic movements of the markets. While it is good practice to check up on your portfolio in regular increments to gauge developments, it is not a good idea to continuously watch and monitor minute-by-minute progress.

I can tell you assuredly, "markets will fluctuate" is the one truth about investing in the markets; your dividend stock portfolio is no exception. So long as you are confident in your due diligence, you are well on your way toward Financial Freedom!

Caveats on a Dividend Investing Strategy

Caveat #1: DRIP Investing is Now Free

Although DRIP is still a fantastic way to have your stock purchases on auto-pilot, it has lost some of its appeal now that most brokerage firms offer fee-free trades.

For example, in the past when you receive a dividend, if you took that dividend as cash and wanted to reinvest it at a later date, you would be subjected to a fee (usually anywhere from $2.95-6.95) to initiate any new position.

This means that if you were receiving $40 in dividends in cash and you later wanted to invest in a new security, a $6.95 fee would represent 17.4% of the dividend ($6.95/$40), rendering the constant repurchasing of new positions cost-prohibitive and making DRIP the better option over cash.

This was because on DRIP, the fee was often waived, so your $40 would become a full $40 purchased position in the stock. This made DRIP very lucrative, especially for smaller investors wanting to build positions quickly.

Trading firms are increasingly offering fee-free trading, which means that you are not subjected to any fees on any stock purchases. I still personally use DRIP investing, but my motivations for doing so have shifted from a money-saving mechanism to a seeing DRIP as a form of 'auto-pilot dollar-cost averaging.'

Caveat #2: 'Set-it and Forget-it' Can Only Take You So Far

Despite DRIP being a fantastic option and our inclination as value investors to a 'buy and hold forever' strategy, we do need to be diligent and follow the companies we are invested in for material changes in operations.

One of the major risks that we run in dividend investing is to truly adopt the 'set-it and forget-it' mindset. A stock could be losing value before our eyes, yet if we keep buying more and more of it, we might be chasing 'bad money' if the worst-case scenario happens: the stock goes to zero.

DivTalk: When you hear someone say a 'stock is going to zero', it generally means that the company is headed towards liquidation or bankruptcy and that soon the overall equity position will be worthless.

If a company begins a downward spiral and the dividend is at risk of being cut, we must make the decision on when/how to sell our positions to maintain the preservation of our hard-earned capital. After all, it is much more difficult to make up gains than it is to make up losses.

DivTalk: As an example of how challenging it can be to make up losses in our investment portfolio, take the following example.

Assume that we have invested $100,000 into the market at varying positions. If that portfolio falls to $50,000, you have suffered a loss of 50% in portfolio value ((100,000-50,000)/100,000).

However, to grow that back to the original $100,000 investment, you would need to make an additional $50,000 on that portfolio, which represents a gain of $50,000, or 100% on the now $50,000 portfolio.

The first priority of an investor is capital preservation as it is a most difficult proposition to make up for losses on principle.

While the goal is to maintain absolute ownership throughout our lifetime, it is important to recognize that we will be wrong in our analysis from time-to-time. It is when we are emotionally detached and cognizant of our potential to be wrong that we are open to changing course when the situation presents itself.

By maintaining diligence in following developments in the positions within our portfolio, we can avoid significant and foreseen losses.

Caveat #3: You Will Battle Machines

In our modern-day age of investing, you must accept the fact that AI trading (artificial intelligence, machine learning) is here to stay. There are currently computer trading programs that will make trades based on algorithms. These 'algos' will make buy and sell decisions within a matter of moments based on a news event that their 'bots' picked from halfway around the world.

I mention this to accentuate the point that the trading world will never be the same. No matter how fast of a trader you become, I can guarantee that you will not be as fast as the algorithmic trading formula down the street.

Ten times out of ten you will lose on speed of execution.

While we cannot win on our quickness of trading, we can win the long-term game. The buy and hold game is never dead, though it gets more challenging in this day and age as technological advances threaten to make companies - and entire industries - obsolete in what seems like a heartbeat.

No matter what new technology comes our way, the key is to know your competition and adapt your strategy accordingly.

Caveat #4: There are Risks in Buying Any Stock, Including Dividend Stocks

Keep in mind that any strategy is subjected to risk of loss and a dividend investing strategy is no different. Many of the companies that we invest in are deemed 'value plays' and might be priced so because their future growth prospects are bleak.

An example of this is the company, Newell Brands ($NWL). This seems to be a well-run company, with very recognizable brands, which happen to be in dying industries. Some of the top brands are Elmers glue and Expo whiteboard markers. Both of these brands are very recognizable and can be found in most homes and classes rooms across the country.

However, it is no surprise that these once iconic and fully-utilized product groups are now at risk of being replaced entirely by computer tablets in classrooms and homes across the country. Will $NWL be able to navigate the waters ahead and steady the ship? Only time can tell.

The goal in finding value plays are to find those companies that are the proverbial "diamonds in the rough." These are the companies that might be undervalued but have a steady stream of cash flow which more than covers the dividend payment.

Anytime we make an investment, we run the risk that the companies we invest in will not generate enough free cash flow to cover their dividend payments and that, inevitably, these same companies will have to cut their dividends. This is the worst-case scenario, though we see it happen time and time again.

If the company has a long history of paying a stable dividend and one day cuts or eliminates the dividend payment, this is a very poor sign. It's not always an automatic sell sign, but it is a major cause for concern.

For each investor, the day will come when you are faced with the decision of whether or not to sell a stock in light of poor news. It becomes less a question of 'if' a stock in their portfolio will cut its dividend, but rather 'when'. The goal is to have a plan in place beforehand so you will know how to react.

While we won't go into massive details around the simple dividend investing strategy here, it's worth repeating: any investment strategy is subject to risks. Know and manage your risk profile!

Dividend Investing Strategy: Implementation

In this section, we'll now get into the nuts and bolts of the Dividend Investing Strategy and begin laying the foundation to implement this strategy.

Keep in mind that buying stocks that pay dividends is no different than buying stocks that do not, it is just that the criteria we utilize will change.

As with any investment strategy, there are many risks inherent to investing and it is up to each investor to know his or her particular risk tolerance level and to make adaptations accordingly.

Learning this strategy will be wild, fun, and more rewarding than you have ever imagined. After all, what is better than cutting out the middleman (your broker) and buying stocks directly from the exchanges themselves?

Even if you don't want to buy up individual shares, you will still be able to buy very low-cost mutual funds or ETF funds that track the markets while maintaining a standard position in each particular company. If that's how you choose to invest, get out there and start buying!

For those who do want to purchase their own individual stocks and follow the heart of the ownership mentality that we preach at MoneyByRamey.com, let's dive into the Strategy in Action.

The Dividend Investing Strategy Steps: Beginning

Investing in individual stocks can be like finding the proverbial "needle in a haystack". It requires sifting through seemingly endless information to arrive at stocks that are ripe for the taking.

Our first task in this dividend investing journey is to develop our 'whys' for deploying our capital. Let's begin with developing our checklist.

Step 1: Develop Your Dividend Checklist

The first, and most important element of the dividend investing strategy, is to develop your dividend checklist. This checklist will be your first ally in the journey of sifting through company after company to discover the ones that match your ideal investment profile.

Keep in mind that your dividend checklist does not have to be the same as my dividend checklist. In fact, I encourage you to develop your own 'flavor' so to speak, as to the stocks you purchase and why you purchase them.

In this step, you can do all sorts of criteria variations and combinations: high risk, low risk, certain exchanges, certain valuations (i.e. market caps), off 52-week highs, off 52-week lows, etc. There are no rules here; we are focused only on what works.

By developing the elements of your dividend checklist, you will begin to craft and refine your own investment strategy.

This step is very important as without understanding yourself and why you invest in the first place, you will be lost in the myriad of investment criteria available to the modern-day investor. It will become the classic 'paralysis by analysis' situation.

Your checklist will become your go-to stock screener for potential investments into dividend-paying stocks. Picture this as your high-level, quick-view tool which tells you whether or not you would consider a company for investment. By having this checklist available, it can save you a lot of time and hassle by only going after stocks when and where your investment criteria are met.

The 7 Elements in My Dividend Checklist

What do I advocate when making this dividend checklist? Simplicity. I personally use my own dividend checklist when I am in my 'QuickView' analysis phase. This simple criteria helps me to know whether or not a stock might be ideal for a deeper dive or if I want to hit the pass button and move on.

In itself, developing your dividend checklist is a great exercise, as it makes an investor have to put down on paper the essential elements of their particular investing strategy. By thinking through our strategy, we can develop the reasons why we invest, and as a result, out subsequent investing becomes that much more refined.

While you will eventually build your own checklist based on your investing experience, I offer the 7 elements in my dividend checklist below.

Element #1: Is There a Moat?

The first thing an investor needs to look for is "does this particular company have a moat?"

What do we mean by the term, 'moat'?

Think back to the ancient castle days. When two factions were at war with one another, the only way to win was to successfully attack and overtake the enemy castle. Opposing forces attempted to breach the castle walls during an ongoing conflict.

The soldiers of the castle needed to figure out ways to make the castle impregnable to breach. Mechanisms, engineer, and designs were completed to make castles as difficult as possible to intrude. One of the very clever ways they did this was through creating a moat, which was a low dug pit, typically filled by water, which surrounded the castle.

In addition to scaling the already-intimidating castle walls, invaders would have the moat barrier to deal with before they were able to attempt scaling the walls of the castle. By having this moat around the castle, the forces inside the castle had another layer of protection from having their castle breached.

Why do I digress to talking about moats in the same breadth as dividend investing?

It's because many companies today deal with competitors looking to dethrone them on a daily basis. Therefore, companies are charged with creating their own competitive advantages which they use to protect themselves from the onslaught of market rivals. These competitive advantages are referred to as moats; those things that the particular company does well that are very hard, if not impossible, for competitors to duplicate.

In looking to deploy your hard-earned capital into a company, one of your first duties as an investor is to figure out what the company's particular moats happen to be.

Typically in large, publicly traded companies, moats will exist to some extent. These moats represent the competitive advantages that are inherent to the particular company (see Michael Porter's Five Forces Analysis for further reading).

These moats, used interchangeably with competitive advantages, can exist in many forms. Here are a few active examples of what I would classify as current-day moats:

- **Microsoft ($MSFT)** It has dominance of the computer software industry. Utilization of its programs is standard practice within many businesses, so switching programs can become problematic. For instance, if you try to send a Google doc or Libreoffice file in the business world, that typically won't work. Many companies will want to see the file in a Microsoft Word (.docx format) as it is the file type they are comfortable with as it is standard on its enterprise platform.

- **Tesla ($TSLA)** Whether you think this is a well-run company or headed towards bankruptcy is beside the point; Tesla has some of the most loyal consumers I have ever seen. Simply visit any public message board regarding this stock and you'll find two things; the bears that argue it cannot go on, and the bulls that think otherwise and keep the stock propped up to great heights. The solid investor support, is a form of a moat.

- **Coke ($KO)** Coke is currently the #1 recognized brand name in the world, which is a truly amazing feat. It has accomplished this through having an iconic product that comes by many decades of solid advertising. Being that it is so recognizable, you can see that Coke has a competitive advantage, as it is very challenging for a beverage competitor to compete with Coke on both the size, scale, and taste of its products. I would personally argue that most people do not buy Coke for the taste, but for the emotions that the first sip of the product brings up in them.

This list of moat examples could go on. The key is not to buy or sell based only on the proposition of competitive advantage; rather your goal in this first step of the dividend checklist is to ascertain if the moat exists in the first place.

Keep in mind that figuring out if a moat exists and what that moat happens to be is a highly subjective process. What one person thinks is a moat might be, in another's eyes, an easily penetrated aspect of the company or industry as a whole.

The key is to keep an open mind, do research, and trust your investment acumen during this stage of the process.

Element #2: Growing or Stable Industry

I like to buy dividends in industries and sectors that are experiencing growth or that I believe are going to experience growth. The big question to ask here is "What are the company/industry growth prospects?"

Out of all the dividend checklist steps, this one is the most subjective. It requires an investor to put on his/her "future goggles" and make some radical assumptions. You don't have to be 100% correct or even 100% convinced; the goal is to be realistic, observe trends, and be confident in your outlook.

At this present time, I own a few companies that have "legacy services". Legacy services have been built up over many years and are typically based on an older product that is coming against headwinds of new technologies. The company is still producing cash flow, but eventually these legacy services will fade away as new technological advances begin to take center stage.

If a company only has legacy services that are cash flowing for them and no future technological prospects to meet the business climate of tomorrow, that would be a candidate that I do not want to invest in as their time is limited and the future prospects are trending downward.

What we have seen is that technology is the great disruptor, and the fact is that in putting our hard-earned capital to work means that we need to make sure that we are buying into companies that are actively growing, or at the very least, stabilized.

Does that mean that in our search for values if we see a revenue stream going down, that we will not invest in that company? Not necessarily.

While I do believe that a decline in revenues is concerning and something that requires a good amount of due diligence to discover a root cause, I believe that the investor needs to look at where the current macro trends are heading as well as how the company is addressing the general disruption.

For instance, a few sectors that I'm very hesitant to invest in right now are gas and oil companies as well as companies that produce unhealthy type of foods. My main objective for not wanting to deploy capital in companies in these industries comes from the fact that I view both of these sectors on downward trajectories.

Personally, I do not believe that oil will be around long-term, and this fact shows itself in the world looking to transition to alternative forms of renewable energy.

Now, does oil significance go away anytime soon? Perhaps not in my lifetime or the lifetime after me, but I still get concerned about oils' lack of ability to transition to new technology.

DivTalk: Despite my reservation about oil long-term, I am still invested in two oil majors: $XOM and $BP. I have added to these positions of late as well, as oil is taking a hit on worldwide recession concerns.

I am banking on the fact that these companies can find a way to transition their breadth of operations to new technologies and processes that can be around long-term. Time will tell if this is the right play.

The same can be said of food companies that dance between healthy and unhealthy options. A trend we are currently seeing is that the world, led by millennials in the United States, is seeking healthier, organic, and environmentally-friendly food products.

More and more companies like Kraft-Heniz ($KHC) are facing head-winds of consumers buying local, buying non-processed, and buying alternative food options.

This isn't to say that companies like Kraft or McDonalds ($MCD) or Coke ($KO) won't make it in this new normal; rather it is that companies need to adapt to market forces and consumer trends in order to keep a positive trajectory moving forward.

Element #3 Stable or Increasing Revenues

Similar to the point above, I like to invest in companies that are growing. Often my focus is on whether a company is growing their top-line sales figure, either through increasing prices or increasing market share.

For the dividend investor, it is very important to see a company tapping new markets or delivering new products to its consumers. As long as a company remains innovative and one step ahead of competitors, its market dominance can continue in the form of winning new customers while continuing to grow its already loyal user base.

However, if a company falls behind competitors or its products fall out of line with the general consumer, the company could be headed for dire times. This trend is often seen in a decline or drop in revenues. It is something for investors to watch closely.

DivTalk: A decline in revenues does not always indicate dire circumstances. For instance, if a company's revenues are largely based on commodity prices, it is not unreasonable to see significant fluctuations in the overall sales figures as prices for commodities rise and fall.

For instance, if a company sells 10,000,000 bushels of corn and the price per bushel is $7.00, the company's revenues are $70,000,000. However, if they sell the same amount of corn - 10,000,000 bu. - but the price drops to $3.50, then the same amount of sales converts to $35,000,000 in revenues.

Does this mean the company is headed for dire times? Not necessarily. As an astute investor, it is your job to analyze any revenue decreases - as well as increases - to ascertain the meaning for the company's future.

Also, in the example above, it would be more beneficial for the investor to look at gross margins to see how well the company is handling its top line revenue against its day-to-day expenses.

If I see that revenues are on a general decline, it tips me off that the company might be struggling with its current product offering or that a competitor is creating disruption in the marketplace. In any case, a decline in revenues certainly requires a more thorough analysis.

Element #4: Positive Cash Flow From Operations

The most important thing for me to see on a company's financial statements are positive cash flow from operations (CFFO). Why is this so important? This metric tells me whether or not the company was able to generate cash from its day-to-day operations. If a company is cash flow positive, the likelihood for them to continue paying dividends quarter-after-quarter, and year-after-year, is higher.

What is cash flow from operations?

Cash Flow From Operations (CFFO), is a reflection of the actual cash generated from the company's everyday business operations. I personally believe that an investor can derive more from the CFFO on the cash flows statement than from net income on the income statement.

This is because net income (NI) is a number that is mainly based on accounting principles and is subject to being manipulated by everyday accounting practices.

I am not saying that accountants are fraudsters. Merely what I am attempting to convey is that accounting income and 'real' cash flow are two different things. This is because the tax law is designed to allow companies to deduct certain expenses to help reduce their tax liability and encourage continued investment into various sectors.

The end result is that companies can reduce their net income through various means, which ends up reducing the amount of tax the company owes when the tax bill comes due. Cash flows are much more resistant to these fluctuations and present a truer sense of the cash flow position.

Take for instance the following example regarding net income vs. cash flow, which has been excerpted from the 12/31/17 3M ($MMM) 10-K:

3M ($MMM) Cash Flow

12/31/17 10-K

Net Income	4,869,000,000
CFFO	6,240,000,000
Difference?	1,371,000,000

Why was there a $1.4B difference between NI and CFFO? The main culprit is a $1.54B depreciation and amortization charge which was added back into the net income in the cash flow section of the 2017 annual report. Why? Because depreciation is not a 'real expense' in the actual definition of the word.

93

Keep in mind that the cash flows statement exists to reconcile the actual inflows and outflows of cash. Since the company didn't incur any real cash outflow for the depreciation expense, then it must recognize depreciation as a non-cash expense. The overall effect then is for depreciation to be added back into the net income figure to demonstrate a more accurate cash flow figure.

DivTalk: Depreciation expense is an important expense for any company. Depreciation is the cost recognition write-down on existing Property, Plant, and Equipment (PPE). Accounting procedures allow companies to recognize that as they use PPE, the value goes down. Depreciation is the method to account for this drop in value.

This is important due to the fact that on the income statement, depreciation is treated as an expense, which is used to reduce taxable income. If a company is continually growing its operations through the purchasing of PPE or acquisitions, it should be able to have a large depreciation expense year-over-year, which it can use to reduce its taxable income significantly.

Does that mean that non-cash expenses are not important to the overall operations? By no means is this true. It is still important for an investor to take into consideration non-cash expenses and how that affects the company's overall financial situation.

However, strictly from an ability to maintain paying dividends on a regular basis, investors want to make sure that they understand how much cash a company actually generates. To determine this, the cash flow statement is vitally important and can be the investor's greatest ally.

In my working experience, I have reviewed financial statements where a company is making a healthy net income and seems to be on solid footing, but when you look into the cash flow statements, the opposite is true.

The company is, in fact, not generating much cash flow which could adversely affect operations if sources of capital dry up. Perhaps the company is using more cash in their operations, not collecting as quickly on receivables, or perhaps another factor which negatively affects cash coming in the door.

This is important for investors to note because if there happens to be any potential issues in a company's cash flow, one of the first payable items to be cut in order to bring a cash-positive situation back in line is the dividend.

Why is this? Because it dividend is a very highly elective payment from a company. Unless the shares are preferred - which require a dividend to be paid and act more as a debt instrument than a security - the company has no legal requirement to pay dividends to shareholders.

Needless to say, a healthy cash flow quarter after quarter is something that I look for when analyzing any stock for a potential investment.

Element #5: Dividends are Covered Through Cash Flow

Once I verify that there has been positive cash flow in the current quarter and in previous years, I then move on to my next high-level metric to make sure that the dividends are covered through cash flow from operations.

The cash flow from operations dividend by dividends

(CFFO/Divs) is a very important metric for me, because if dividends are not being covered by the company's cash flow, then I can only wonder where the cash is coming from to pay for those dividends.

The answer can always be found in the cash flow statement itself. If a company lacks the cash flow to cover its dividend payment, it will take on some form of debt financing or additional share issuance in order to pay for dividends.

If this increase in company debt or share float happens to be a one-time, one-off occurrence, then I might not be as concerned. However if we see the company routinely financing its dividend through issuing more debt or common shares, then this should be seen as a negative trend and one that should be cause for much deeper investigation.

Therefore, it is very important to see that dividends are being paid through cash that the company is generating quarter after quarter. Here I would like to adapt an old saying to our checklist element; "Cashflow is truly King."

Element #6: Positive Working Capital for the Past Three to Five Years

Once I ascertain that the company has the cash flow to meet dividend payments, I then want to move on to the liquidity of the company.

DivTalk: Liquidity is the amount of cash or cash-like items that a company has on hand. This is an important metric to me because having good liquidity is directly related to the company's ability to meet its debt obligations.

The term, 'stay liquid' means to keep enough cash on hand.

> While we don't want the companies we invest in to hold profits in only cash as it loses value due to inflation, we want them to be conservative with their money rather than overly aggressive.
>
> The goal for individuals - and companies alike - is to keep enough cash on hand to meet any necessary current obligations as well as unforeseen expenses, and then to invest the rest.

Personally, I know how important it is to have cash on hand to be able to meet day-to-day debt obligations. Therefore, when I'm looking at companies that are paying dividends, I want to make sure that they have the general liquidity to handle their day-to-day obligations.

I tend to get concerned if I see a negative working capital ratio or position, as this tells me that the company, if they had to liquidate all of their current assets today, could not pay for all their current liabilities and would either need to borrow more and cut expenses to meet payments to vendors.

For a dividend paying company, one of the big liabilities that the company elects to pay is the quarterly dividend. This can be found on the balance sheet in the form of dividends payable.

Being that this is a highly elective payable for a company, it is likely that if the company were to come into a cash flow crunch, one of the first expenses to be cut would be the dividend payable. Since I am an investor who is focused solely on my annual dividend income, I would not like to see a dividend being cut as this directly cuts into my yearly income. More often than not when I see a dividend cut or about to be cut, I see it as a sell signal.

This is not always 100%, but I have found that more often than not, companies with a negative working capital position eventually struggle to pay the dividend. This is why I chose this element as a metric in my dividend checklist.

Element #7: Debt/Equity At or Close to 1x

Another important metric for me when reviewing a stock for purchase is that the company is not over-leveraged. I have seen too many companies take on enormous amounts of debt, only to be paving their way toward oblivion when the generally economy, and themselves by extension, reach rough times. This is why I like to dial in on companies with a debt ratio at or near a 1x multiple.

To figure out this ratio, I do a simple calculation which includes all debt, both current and long-term. I simply take Total Debt / Total Equity. This gives me a high-level overview of the company's leverage situation.

Why is this so important? Debt is like the classic "mountain under the sea" scenario. When the water is high and plentiful, the sailing ship does not care nor does it even notice the mountain that lurks below. However, once the water begins to recede, the ship is in danger of striking the mountain.

The same thing can be seen with companies that carry enormous amounts of debt. While the company's cash flow is high and the overall economy is doing well, then debt does not seem to be a problem. However, once the economy hits a rough patch or the company goes through trying times, that debt then becomes like the mountain beneath the sea, ever ready to slice the bow of the ship with its serrated tip.

Call me old school, but I like more conservative companies. Companies that are more debt-averse and seek out growth through cash flow are much more appealing to me than companies that are taking on enormous debt to achieve a growth trajectory that might not be sustainable.

I do have companies in my portfolio with debt levels that are higher, but for me, if a company has too much debt, it is a sure sign to walk away. Be careful of over leveraging as nothing could ever tank a dividend payer quicker than a company mired in debt.

Now that we have seen the 7 elements of a dividend checklist, we'll move onto step 2 of the dividend investing strategy.

Step 2: Develop Your Criteria

Developing your stock criteria is very important in your dividend investing journey. This general criteria will be what drives you entire investing strategy. It will take some trial and error to develop the various metrics you utilize each time you screen stocks, but it will be well worth it in the long run to lay the foundation for your investment process.

DivTalk: Developing your criteria comes after creating your dividend checklist, mainly because the criteria takes longer to develop and is usually learned over a lifetime of investing. Both of the steps can and should be done in tandem, and then refined over the course of one's investing life.

Keep in mind that there is no right or wrong way to develop criteria. The only test that your personal criteria must pass are:

- Does it perform?

- Are your pre-defined metrics matching or beating the general market returns?

- Are they providing you the type of investment performance which you seek?

It will take some time to discover this information. When beginning, it is often a good idea to create a 'mock portfolio' to test out your strategy. A mock portfolio would include purchasing stocks just like you normally would, with the only difference being that you are not using real money, but rather simulating without actually buying any stock. Mimic how you would normally purchase (i.e. $2k increments, every Friday, large caps, etc.) and see how your criteria performs.

Remember too - you can always tweak based on performance or observation. Perhaps the market is on a bull run and you want to loosen up on your debt ratio to have more companies show up on your screener. That is all fine and dandy so long as you know the risks inherent to buying companies with larger debt loads.

Over the years, I have fine tuned my own investment criteria. These have changed and developed as I gather more information and see performance trends. By doing so, I have developed my ideal criteria for investments into dividend paying stocks.

Here are the MoneyByRamey.com Dividend Criteria:

- 3%+ Div Yield

- $5B+ Market Cap

- Listed on a US Stock Exchange

- Price/Earnings (PE) Ratio Less than 20x

- Debt/Equity Ratio Less than 2x

- 15+ years consistent dividend payments

These are my starting points for when I dive into stocks. How do I find these stocks? The best method is the utilization of stock screening tools.

Step 3: Find Your Stocks via Screeners

Next up after defining your dividend checklist and your criteria for investment is to find your stocks. Finding the right stock to invest in among the multitude of choices available is much like the 'needle in a haystack' proposition. There are so many choices that often times investors can get bogged down in this step.

Stock screeners are important to this process as they allow you to sort and filter the myriad of publicly traded stocks to match your already-defined criteria for investment. A good screener ensures that the needle is easier to find by making the haystack much smaller.

For stock screeners, I recommend a multitude of tools. I personally have a go-to stock screeners that I use, which I combine with my own proprietary Google sheets screener which live tracks the companies that I am following. In addition to this, I follow other authors, investors, and writers to get new investment ideas on a daily basis.

Best Stock Screeners

There are programs and websites out there that will help you in your dividend investing journey. These are known as 'screeners'. The basic premise of these screeners is that you insert criteria that you want to screen for and the site will return stocks that fit those various data points. Here is an example of what the FinViz.com screener looks like:

source: www.finviz.com

I find these screeners very helpful for sorting by initial criteria to find stocks worthy of investing your hard-earned capital. Keep in mind though that the screener is just a tool to help identify potential stocks and should not be seen as the final word on whether or not a stock should be invested in. More due diligence should be done in order to determine if a stock is worthy of investment.

Here are some Stock Screeners that I utilize:

- **FinViz.com** - this site has a great tool which allows you to query off of various metrics. I find it is a great place to begin a journey of finding great dividend stocks.

- **SeekingAlpha.com** - SA does not have a screening tool per se, but I find that it offers some great insights into companies and has a good dividend analysis tool. I couple SA with FinViz to find out more information on the dividend.

- **Google Finance** - While Google Finance has changed around their screening tool, I still find it is a good place to draw information from. I don't use it as much as I used to for screening purposes, but I do utilize its API in developing my own tracker.

Develop Your Own Tool

Another option which is beyond the scope of this book is to develop your own screening tool. I find that the customization of building your own screener program is certainly helpful in a journey towards managing a dividend portfolio.

You can utilize Google or other API service to build your own tool in sheets or Excel. Be on the lookout for MoneyByRamey.com to roll out a dividend tracking software or website in the coming months or years ahead to better help you manage your portfolio.

Follow Others Who Invest in Stocks

I also find great ideas by following and reading other's contents. There are a ton of great bloggers and financial writers out there, with many of them focusing on dividend investing. Go out, begin reading the ideas and materials that others produce.

The goal is to be a sponge and learn as much as you can to continue to hone your own investment strategy. Who knows, you might also find a dividend-paying company to invest in that you hadn't thought of before.

Some great places that I go to find others with investment ideas:

- SeekingAlpha.com
- StockTwits.com
- Marketwatch.com
- Yahoo Finance
- Google Finance
- Following others across media platforms

If you are on social media, I find that a great place to start is with a hashtag or search on your topic of choice. Being a dividend investor that utilizes Twitter, I often will search for #dividend in the search field, which brings up a ton of articles written on recent purchases. This is a fun way to interact with others and see what other individual investors are buying into.

Step 4: Engage in the Deep Dive

Next up after finding stocks on your screener is to engage in "the Deep Dive".

In the deep dive process, your goal is to become a relative expert in the various companies you are looking to invest in. I say relative because I do not want you to get lost in the countless minuta of data available. You could spend the rest of your life studying up on the 10-Ks, 10-Qs, 8-Ks, etc. of the companies you are looking to invest in, but that is not the end goal. We have to stay out of 'analysis paralysis' territory.

Rather the overarching due diligence goal is to become very knowledgeable on what the company does and whether or not it will be a company worthy of investing your hard-earned capital.

In the Deep Dive process, our goal will be to build up a solid level of understanding into what a company does to earn its income on a daily basis. By ensuring that we know and understand the company's overall operations, we will be setting ourselves up for success in our investment portfolios.

Here is a general list of the questions we want to answer in our Deep Dive process:

- What does the company do on a daily basis?

- What are its business units?

- How does the company earn its income?

- How do I feel about the company's overall financial situation?

- What is the outlook for the company?

- What is the outlook for the company's industry?

- Who are the company's competitors and how does it stack up?

- What are the analysts saying about this company?

- Are any other noteworthy investors investing in this company?

- Who are the institutional owners (if any)?

- What are the short positions and what % of outstanding shares are sold short?

- What are the financial numbers and ratios telling you about this company's future growth prospects?

- Which way is the company's income statement, balance sheet, and cash flows trending?

- How do the financial ratios stack up to historical industry benchmarks, and to that of competitors?

- What is the company's debt load and what are lenders charging for interest?

- What are the debt ratings on this company?

Keep in mind these are only a few of the many questions you are seeking to answer. You might not have to ask all of these; perhaps your understanding will be solidified once you have a few of the key questions answered.

To find the answers to these questions, we can utilize a multitude of tools. Here are a few of my favorites to help complete my Deep Dive. In the spirit of this section, we'll go a little bit deeper into each tool to explain how and why I use it:

Finviz.com

This is one of my top sites for holding my portfolio and doing overall research. I love their initial screener tool; outside of my own custom-built screener, the Finviz screener is the one that I use the most.

I find that the information on various stocks is very solid and intuitive. The charts are very easy to work with and the various ratios are presented in an easy-to-understand and manageable fashion. In fact, I found an app that allows me to present their chart data on my website, and I'm very happy with the seamlessness of the process and the beauty of the charts.

Best of all, the site presents much of its data for free. This is is always an added benefit for an investor like myself. They do have a monthly paid service, which I have personally never used, so I cannot attest to the value of the service. Knowing how good Finviz is, I'm sure this service is well worth the monthly outlay.

SeekingAlpha.com

SeekingAlpha is another great site where I get a lot of investing ideas from solid investors and analysts. SA contains many authors which conduct extensive analysis on various stocks and publish their ideas for the world to read.

The thing that sets SA apart from other sites is that anyone can write an article. You would think that analysis might suffer from this, but I would almost argue that the value of having everyday investors writing about their strategies is even more valuable than reading the usual drudge from market experts. SA also has a team of editors that do a very good job of assuring that only well-written content is allowed to be posted on the site.

SeekingAlpha is more akin to a tight-nit investing community which shares ideas about investing in stocks and wealth generation. The authors typically specialize in certain niches; i.e. dividends, growth stocks, value stocks, or certain companies. This allows for interesting takeaways for everyday readers.

Of interesting note is that I almost get more value from the reading the comments section rather than the author's actual article. Many times the readers will offer insightful thoughts on a particular stock which gives me something more to ponder.

SA also has some useful analysis tools, particularly useful for dividend investors. The dividend section for each particular stock is very well done. There are also many years of analysis which can help investors see the long history of financial data for particular stocks. Beyond this, I do not really use many SA metrics, as I get pretty much everything I need ratio-wise from Finviz.

The biggest knock against SA is that they are going to many subscription-only features in an attempt to make the site profitable. This creates some issues when you visit the site and realize your most-used feature now resides behind a pay wall.

MarketWatch.com

Marketwatch.com is my initial go-to site for the high-level analysis of a company's financials. I find that their summary financial statements are best suited for a Quickview, 50,000 foot view as to where the company is at and which direction it is trending.

Often times I will begin at FinViz, see a stock's chart and ratios, then hop over to Marketwatch to get a good analysis of the financial picture. While scrolling down the page, I will begin to calculate ratios in my head, and ensure that what I was seeing actually meshes with what I'd like to see from a potential investment perspective.

SEC.gov

SEC.gov is my go-to site for really understanding a stock. Since all publicly traded companies are required to produce financial statements four times a year (quarterly), with one of those statements comprising the annual report, it is a bastion of information for the everyday investor.

Not only are the financial figures included in the annual report, but so is pertinent information behind those numbers. The various companies and their management teams will discuss anything that is material to the stock's overall condition. This means they will go into detail regarding the company's outstanding debt, future outlook, revenue segment breakdown, and much more. This type of information is all "gold" in an investor's analysis.

Also found on SEC.gov are any announcements that are material to the stock's operations. For instance, if key directors are selling stock, they must file a report detailing how much and when they are selling. While I do not recommend that investors pour through reports other than

10-Ks and 10-Qs, there are websites that track this other reportable information and share it with visitors.

Moody's, S&P, and Fitch

In a previous career, I became familiar with the large debt rating agencies, Moody's, S&P, and Fitch. These ratings companies provide an analysis scorecard on the overall debt picture of publicly traded company's bond offerings.

This is important information as it shows the rating of each individual company, ranging anywhere from investment grade to junk grade. Investors can use this information to better ascertain how risky a proposed investment truly is. Keep in mind that the ratings agencies are largely human-driven and can be prone to make mistakes (such as not predicting the mortgage meltdown). Remember that all of these are only small tools in the investor's overall arsenal.

These agencies also offer ratings on countries, which is of particular importance if you are looking to invest money outside of your current location. I've used these country ratings to help me better determine what countries are ideal for me to do business, and what countries to avoid.

Analyst & General Opinions

Last but not least, I find good value in analyst's opinions and user comments. It is helpful to see whether or not a stock has been downgraded in the eyes or the analysts or to see what the general market has to say about the stock.

I find a lot of good analyst upgrade/downgrade information on Finviz.com in the chart section for each stock. I also like the Finviz page because it contains a feed of recent news articles pertaining to the particular stock as well as a Stocktwits feed laying out the latest user-generated commentary.

The list of great sources of information is vast and can change as new tools are built and discovered. I do not always utilize each tool mentioned above when conducting a deep dive, however, it is good to know what is available to me. Anytime a great new tool becomes available, I will look to utilize it in my research process. Likewise, if a tool becomes obsolete or ineffective, it will be time to replace it.

In the next section, I will layout an example of the deep dive process in action and how I go about finding answers to the stock's underlying value utilizing the tools outlined here.

Once we have completed our deep dive analysis, it is finally time to answer the question: to invest or not to invest?

Step 5: Invest or Not to Invest!

Here is where all of the analysis comes to a head: it is finally time to answer the question, "Do I 'pull the trigger' and deploy capital into the stock? Or do I hold off and wait for a better value entry point or look to invest in a different stock entirely?"

Keep in mind that we won't always buy in at the correct time.

We will sometimes buy high, only to see the stock go down.

We will sometimes buy low, and see our stock rise to new heights.

The important thing is to make solid decisions based on proper valuation metrics. So long as we make an entry at a good price point in a great company, we can rest assured that our decision was the right one.

Remember that our goal with a dividend investing strategy is to focus less on the everyday inherent fluctuations of the market as a whole, but rather to be focused on our annual dividend income. So long as the ADI is heading in an upward trajectory and our stocks are not deteriorating from an overall financial perspective, then all is good.

In fact, as dividend investors, a market decline should be a welcomed scenario as it allows us to buy more of our favorite dividend payers at lower prices. No matter if we're buying through cash or DRIP, the result is the same; more stock ownership and more dividends.

This is the Snowball Effect in action.

Now that we have bought our stock, it is now time to track our purchase, both for tax and performance purposes.

Step 6: Buy & Track Your Purchase

Congrats! You made the decision to buy a stock! Your goal now is to keep track of your entry point and track its performance. For this step, you can utilize a myriad of free tools available or you can build your own spreadsheet tracker. I personally advocate doing both.

If you do not have the time or the desire to build your own tracking system, then you can easily find tools available, many of them are offered for free or at a low cost. I currently track my stocks on a few different websites, mainly because I like being able to view my data in different ways. I find that each tool has its strengths and weaknesses, so by leveraging my data across different websites, I am able to find exactly what it is I am looking for.

Here is where I currently track my portfolios:

- My own personal custom-built screener

- Finviz.com

- SeekingAlpha.com

- Nasdaq.com

- StockTwits.com

When first starting out, I always advocate simplicity - you can start with tracking in one website, learn all the nuances in their tracking tool, then move onto other tools from there.

The goals of tracking your purchases is two-fold:

- **Track your stock's overall performance** - This would include tracking gain/loss, overall percentage of the portfolio, annual dividend income, and any other metric you might find pertinent

- **To maintain a cost basis for tax reporting purposes** - When you file your taxes, you will need to know how much dividend income you received and, if you happen to sell a stock during a tax year, the cost basis for your purchases. This can get rather complicated very fast, so make sure to thoroughly read up on this topic or hire a competent professional to help you along the way!

The Strategy In ACTION!

Now that you understand the basics of the strategy, we will go through the process of choosing potential dividend stocks for investment. I'll take you through some different stocks to see exactly what I look for when considering a potential investment into these dividend payers.

We'll be doing the Quickview on all four stocks and a Deep Dive into one company.

DivTalk: Remember that you can always visit MoneyByRamey.com for more analysis on stocks! We're continually buying into new positions and analyzing stocks to help you in your journey towards Financial Freedom, especially through building up your passive income with dividend investing.

When viewing stocks in our screener tools, we are targeting stocks with the following criteria:

- 3%+ dividend yield
- $5B+ market cap
- PE Ratio less than 20x
- Traded on a US stock exchange

DivTalk: I do invest in foreign stocks on occasion, but it is not my bread and butter. I typically buy into US companies as I know those markets better. There is nothing keeping you from diversifying outside of the US though; just make sure

---

you know why you are choosing those particular countries that you are screening.

Keep in mind that you can tweak this criteria as you see fit; for my current investing strategy, these criteria represent my personal 'sweet spot'.

For each stock we analyze, we will look to complete the following dividend analysis phases:

1. **Calculate Forward Dividend Income**

2. **The Quickview**

   a. **Is a moat present?**

   b. **Is the CFFO positive?**

   c. **Did CFFO cover dividend payments?**

   d. **Was working capital positive the past 3-5 years?**

   e. **Is the company in a growing industry?**

   f. **Is the debt/equity at, close to, or under 1x?**

3. **The Spread**

4. **The Deep Dive**

5. **Buy?**

For the first three stocks, we'll take the stock up to The Spread process, and on the last stock, we'll take it through the deep dive process to get a better understanding of what the numbers are really telling us.

Let's get started on analyzing the first stock.

Caterpillar ($CAT) Dividend Analysis

With stocks being beaten up over the Chinese tariff war news, Caterpillar has become an interesting stock to watch. Since its roots are big into the worldwide manufacturing and construction industry, any slow downs in those sectors could mean slowdowns for CAT as a whole.

This trend has been driving its stock to trading off of 52 week lows, but has also presented an opportunity to capture this stock at a lower price, which has pushed the dividend yield up past the 3% mark.

For our first example, we'll look into the case for a potential investment into CAT.

#1 - Forward Dividend Income

As the first step in our dividend analysis process, we always look to calculate the forward dividend income. We do this by entering the data into the forward dividend calculator. Here are the results for CAT:

Forward Dividend Calculator

Investment Amount	$5,000.00
Stock Ticker	CAT
Share Price	$114.06
Dividend	$1.03
Dividend Frequency	4
Annual Dividend Payout	$4.12
Shares Purchased	43.8
Payout/Yr.	$180.61
Payout/Qtr.	$45.15
Yield	3.61%
Share Accumulation	1.58

As we can see by the calculator's results, this is beginning to look like an interesting opportunity to own a good company at an affordable entry point. The fact that the dividend yield is above 3% when it has been trending in the 1-2% range the past few years is a positive sign for a dividend value investor.

The only drawback that I can see is that at or near the stock price level of $119, I would only accumulate a little over a share per year with this stock on DRIP. Ideally the goal is to have that accumulation be higher, but the caveat is that typically the higher the share accumulation, the higher the overall risk on the stock. As investors, we need to balance this risk/reward scenario carefully.

Being that the FDI is intriguing, it is enough for me to take the stock into the next round of our review: the Quickview.

#2 - The Quickview

Here we will complete the 'eyeball' test, and quickly compute these factors in our head or answers these questions as best as we can.

For those of you that are detail-oriented, you can always complete the Spread before answering the questions in the Quickview phase, however I find that stocks do not always pass the questioned answered below, thus making the entering of the data into the Spread irrelevant. Therefore I choose the quick analysis before doing additional work.

    1. Is a moat present?

Yes. Considering that CAT produces many large industrial construction vehicles and equipment, its business model can be very difficult to replicate.

Not only would a competing company need to have significant working capital to begin operations, it would also need the engineering expertise to build such large scale machinery.

In addition to selling machinery, it also has the distribution network to sell its products throughout the world.

2. Is the CFFO positive?

Yes. For 6/30/2019, the cash flow was at $3.7B. This is great to see, but we want to ensure this isn't a one-time, cyclical event. Thus, we'll go over to MarketWatch to see five year annual statement data trends.

A quick look at the company's five year cash flow statement shows that it has had $5.61B+ in positive cash flow. For the dividend investor, this is a good and needed sign, as we want to ensure that the companies we invest in continue to generate solid cash flows with which they can payout dividends.

3. Did CFFO cover dividend payments?

Yes. With CFFO at a solid $3.7B, dividend payments of $986M for 6/30/19 were adequately covered with the cash generated by operations.

This same trend holds true for the annual financial statements as well.

4. Was working capital positive the past three years?

Yes. For this ratio, we will view the balance sheet for the past three fiscal years, which shows current assets around $38B, which covered current liabilities of $28B nicely. It looks as though for the past 3-5 years, the working capital coverage is around $10B.

The one caveat to this ratio specific to Caterpillar is that much of the working capital is made up of inventories, which consists of large construction equipment for sale. Being that these products are not turned over as quickly as say, an iPhone, the positive working capital can be a deceiving number.

We will still answer 'yes', since working capital is positive, but we have to realize that the company would be more susceptible to downturns in the overall market conditions due to having inventory that is not very liquid due to not selling very quickly.

5. Is the company in a growing industry?

Yes. Overall, the company seems to be in a growth phase. While revenues did dip to $38.5B in 2016, it went back up to $54.7B in 2018.

With the current China/US trade war, this will be something to watch for. The company is especially susceptible to any recession that would negatively impact the construction industry.

6. Is the debt/equity at, close to, or under 1x?

No. All of those big machines are not going to finance themselves. With $64B of total debt and $14B of equity, the debt/equity ratio is a bit higher than I'd like to see at 4.6x. This is the biggest knock that I have seen against many modern company - high levels of debt.

Since quantitative easing has made it very cheap for companies to borrow money, I do not blame them for taking advantage of the low interest rate environment to borrow more debt to increase their return on investment.

However, one thing for the astute investor to watch for is the effect this debt has on overall operations. From what I have seen, many companies are using increasing debt positions to hide operational problems within their companies.

Now that CAT has passed the QuickView, we take the stock into the next step in the process: The Spread.

#3 - The Spread

Now it is time for the CAT spread.

Here are four main sections that are calculated:

High-Level Summary Information

	6/30/2019	6 mos.
High Level #s		
P/E Ratio		11.59
MC		$65,052,164,524
Equity		$14,878,000,000
P/B		4.37
Liabilities		$64,309,000,000
Debt/Equity		4.32
Debt/BV		9.27
Working Capital		$12,054,000,000
Working Capital Ratio		1.43

The High-Level Summary Section Highlights:

- Even though the stock's price has been falling, the P/B is a bit higher at 4x. As a value investor, this tells me that we are buying in for 4x the equity of the business.

- Debt ratios are a bit higher than I'd like to see. Since the company makes large industrial equipment highly dependent on the construction sector, this will be something to analyze a bit deeper to see if it is a trend that we are okay with seeing.

The Balance Sheet

Balance Sheet

Current Assets	39,789,000,000
Cash, A/R	7,429,000,000
PPE	13,172,000,000
Total Assets	79,187,000,000
Current Liabilities	27,735,000,000
Long-term Liabilities	36,574,000,000
Total Liabilities	64,309,000,000
Equity	14,878,000,000
Intangible Assets	7,944,000,000
Book Value	6,934,000,000
Working Capital	12,054,000,000
Working Capital ratio	1.43
Debt/Equity ratio	4.32
Debt/BV	9.27

The Balance Sheet Highlights:

- Current assets exceed current liabilities, which is excellent to see. It would be wise to complete a deep dive as we will need to ascertain what assets make up the current amounts. I would be concerned if the equipment for sale was included in these numbers as the large industrial equipment would not be very liquid during a market downturn.

- Intangible assets at $7.9B stands out. I would dig into this a bit more during the deep dive process to figure out what this number consists of. It would be worth it to understand this a bit further.

The Income Statement

Income Statement

Sales	27,898,000,000
COGS	23,478,000,000
Gross Profit	4,420,000,000
Interest Expense	206,000,000
Net Income	3,501,000,000
Depreciation & Amortization	1,288,000,000
Taxes	952,000,000
EBITDA	5,947,000,000
Profit Margin	12.55%
EBITDA/Int Exp	28.87
NI/Int Exp	17.00

The Income Statement Highlights:

- Solid net income which covers interest expense at 17x. This tells me the company makes more than enough profit to cover its debt and that the interest rates on that debt should be relatively low.

The Cash Flow Statement

Cash Flow Statement

CFFO	3,709,000,000
CFFI	(1,079,000,000)
CFFF	(3,051,000,000)
Change in Cash	(421,000,000)
Divs	986,000,000
CFFO/Divs	3.76

The Cash Flow Highlights:

- At a 4x CFFO/Div coverage ratio, everything this looking solid with the CFFO statement. I do not have any concerns at this time about the company's ability to generate solid cash from its operations.

The Spread Summary: CAT

Overall CAT is a solid income and cash flow generator. It shows that even in a tough environment - the Chinese Tariff war world - it can still general solid cash flow and income which cover both dividends and interest expense.

A concern is the company's debt ratio. It is higher than I'd like to see. Some of this happens to do with the type of equipment the company manufactures; large industrial equipment which closely follows the construction industry.

Even though the stock currently trades in the three digit

territory, the dividend yield is enticing at 3.61%. This is definitely a stock that I would consider investing in at this present time.

WestRock ($WRK) Dividend Analysis

The next stock we will analyze is one of my new favorite dividend-paying stocks: WestRock.

Why WestRock?

I personally like their business model. Certainly they are highly dependent on an industry that is currently in decline, the paper industry.

However, they have a great niche in their particular industry of food, beverage, and miscellaneous packaging services. In particular, I see that the beverage industry on an upswing.

I see millennials driving the desire for craft beers and WestRock is certainly a company that can capitalize on that market trend. In fact, a recent article in MarketWatch explained that millennials spend more on craft beer purchases than they do on their cell phone bills (2).

It is trends like this that lead me to believe that WestRock can positively benefit from shifting consumer tastes by packaging more products.

#1 - Forward Dividend Income

Forward Dividend Calculator

Investment Amount	$5,000.00
Stock Ticker	WRK
Share Price	$34.18
Dividend	$0.46
Dividend Frequency	4
Annual Dividend Payout	$1.82
Shares Purchased	146.3
Payout/Yr.	$266.24
Payout/Qtr.	$66.56
Yield	5.32%
Share Accumulation	7.79

Here the share accumulation is certainly on par with what I like to see. At a $5,000 share entry point, I can accumulate nearly eight new shares of stock per year. This means that each year, I will be growing my dividend income by $14.56 (8 new shares * $1.82 current dividend payout). This represents a raise in every sense of the word, just for simply being a shareholder.

Since the FDI picture presents a great opportunity, it is time to complete the Quickview.

#2 - The Quickview

1. Is a moat present?

Yes/No. Here is where I am mixed with WestRock. While the technology and facilities required to turn recycled paper and cardboard into reusable packaging products is certainly quite sophisticated, I do not see it being a competitive advantage.

While it would take a large amount of capital to get into the business, I do not see any special advantage to setting up an operation in this industry. I'm sure there is a certain amount of design and product advantage, but it seems to be a commodity-based industry that could be based around, "who can deliver the best product at the lowest prices?"

Overall though, the capital intensive nature and technology required to launch a manufacturing facility leads me to cite this company as having a decent competitive advantage due to barriers to entry.

2. Is the CFFO positive?

Yes. WestRock makes a good amount of cash flow. A quick look at the 9 mo. 6/30/19 numbers shows that the company generated $1.4B in cash flow from operations. This was mainly due to a solid net income and a large amount of amortization and depreciation expense.

3. Did CFFO cover dividend payments?

Yes. Considering that dividends were $350M, the CFFO/Div ratio was covered at a reasonable 4x. Considering that CAPEX was at $977M, the dividend was still covered by the cash generated from operations.

4. Was working capital positive the past three years?

Yes. A quick look at the past few annual reports shows that working capital was positive. For the most recent available year-end, 9/30/18, the current assets were $4.79B while the current liabilities were $3.33B.

The quarterly reports shows the exact same positive working capital, which is great to see as a dividend investor. If we were doing a deep dive on this stock, we would definitely want to look at what made up both the current assets and current liabilities to ascertain the liquidity and viability of the assets.

5. Is the company in a growing industry?

Yes/No. This is another section where I am currently mixed. The biggest concern is that it is an industry based around the paper sector, which is in obvious decline. While I do not have a positive outlook for the paper sector, I am quite confident in the packaging sector, mainly due to the popularity of beers and the need of food as well as the trends towards more recyclable materials.

The results can be seen in WestRock's top line revenues the past few years, which have been on the rise year-after-year, quarter-after-quarter.

6. Is the debt/equity at, close to, or under 1x?

Yes. The overall debt/equity ratio is at 1.6x, which is well under the 2x that we are generally targeting.

However, much of the equity is made up of $11B of intangible assets, mostly from acquisitions the company has completed in years past. As we are seeing in recent trends, we'll have to keep our eyes on how well these intangible assets are performing as large write-downs can have disastrous consequences on the company's financial situation, and therefore its stock price.

As it stands, the debt picture is acceptable especially if it is being incurred in a low interest rate environment and the company has adequate cash flow to service that debt.

#3 - The Spread

Now it is time to complete the Spread on WestRock, which will give us a good look into whether or not we want to take this stock into the final step of analysis: the Deep Dive.

High-Level Summary Information

High Level #s	6/30/2019	9 mos.
P/E Ratio		12.06
MC		$8,795,949,638
Equity		$11,842,000,000
P/B		0.74
Liabilities		$18,970,000,000
Debt/Equity		1.60
Debt/BV		54.83
Working Capital		$1,604,000,000
Working Capital Ratio		1.45

The High-Level Summary Section Highlights:

- At 12x, current PE ratio is within the range of stocks we target.

- The company has a $9B market cap, which is ideal for what we seek.

- P/B stands for price/book (Market cap/Equity), and tells us that the company is currently valued for less than the overall equity of the business.

- Debt/Equity is favorable at 1.6x, though the debt/BV is very high at 55x. This will require more research should we take this stock into the Deep Dive process.

- Working capital is positive and the ratio is above 1, which is what we want to see.

The Balance Sheet

Balance Sheet

Current Assets	5,194,000,000
Cash, A/R	179,000,000
PPE	11,169,000,000
Total Assets	30,812,000,000
Current Liabilities	3,590,000,000
Long-term Liabilities	15,380,000,000
Total Liabilities	18,970,000,000
Equity	11,842,000,000
Intangible Assets	11,496,000,000
Book Value	346,000,000
Working Capital	1,604,000,000
Working Capital ratio	1.45
Debt/Equity ratio	1.60
Debt/BV	54.83

The Balance Sheet Highlights:

- Debt/Equity in line with my investing norms at 1.6x

- Intangible assets make up a very large portion of the asset and equity base. More due diligence will need to be completed on the intangible assets to ensure that the valuation of these assets remain in place.

The Income Statement

Income Statement	1,000,000
Sales	13,637,000,000
COGS	10,967,000,000
Gross Profit	2,670,000,000
Interest Expense	317,000,000
Net Income	552,000,000
Depreciation & Amortization	1,128,000,000
Taxes	188,000,000
EBITDA	2,185,000,000
Profit Margin	4.05%
EBITDA/Int Exp	6.89
NI/Int Exp	1.74

The Income Statement Highlights:

- Net Income covers expense by only 1.74x. Ideally I'd like this to be higher - this will be something to watch for in the Deep Dive process.

- EBITDA is solid at $2.2B, mainly because the company has a lot of depreciation expense. This is important as the company generates a lot more cash flow than is reported on the income statement.

The Cash Flow Statement

Cash Flow Statement

CFFO	1,400,000,000
CFFI	(4,200,000,000)
CFFF	2,340,000,000
Change in Cash	(460,000,000)
Divs	351,000,000
CFFO/Divs	3.99

The Cash Flow Statement Highlights:

● Dividends are covered by CFFO nicely at 4x.

● The Cash Flows From Investing are a large negative number; it looks to be an acquisition completed during the year. This will be something to research more in the Deep Dive.

The Spread Summary: WRK

Overall WRK is in a good overall position to deploy hard-earned capital. It generates great cash flow which covers dividends nicely, has a pretty solid balance sheet, and the company is growing its top line revenue year-over-year.

Based on the Quickview and Spread process, I would consider this company to be a solid buy proposition for the MoneyByRamey.com dividend portfolio. This is a stock that I would consider taking into the Deep Dive process.

Starbucks ($SBUX) Dividend Analysis

Starbucks is a stock that I added into my portfolio is mid-2018 and has been a great performing position ever since. While the case for its dividend-paying prowess may have dwindled with its stock price going up, it still remains a stock with solid growth potential.

It is my contention that everyone needs their coffee. We've seen the popularity of this drink continue to rise and I believe that trend will continue, especially in the developed worlds. Many companies are looking to make the foray into this sector in order to diversify their operations. We saw this come to fruition when Coke purchased Costa (3).

Starbucks is set up well to serve the coffee needs of the world. With 25,000+ stores worldwide, the coffee giant is well positioned to serve this growing market segment.

Just walk into any Starbucks store and you'll usually see a hub of hustle and bustle. The stores are brimming with activity and many individuals are waiting for their morning cup of 'joe'. And now with the ability to order online ahead of time, many individuals are skipping the dreaded coffee lines and getting their cups to go.

These awesome indicators are enough for me to put this stock through the dividend buying process.

#1 - Calculate Forward Dividend Income

Forward Dividend Calculator

Investment Amount	$5,000.00
Stock Ticker	SBUX
Share Price	$96.56
Dividend	$0.36
Dividend Frequency	4
Annual Dividend Payout	$1.44
Shares Purchased	51.8
Payout/Yr.	$74.57
Payout/Qtr.	$18.64
Yield	1.49%
Share Accumulation	0.77

In getting a glimpse at the 1.49% dividend yield for Starbucks, it is below the typical 3% I seek for investments into dividend-paying stocks. The case for the ADI is not quite there either, as this entry point into SBUX would net us around an extra share accumulation per year.

When I purchased this stock a year ago, it was closer to the 3% dividend yield with a decent case for share accumulation. The stock is now up over 50% year-to-date, so it has been a solid performer on the capital gains side, which has caused it to lack from the share accumulation perspective.

This fall off in both dividend yield and share accumulation might be enough for me to pass on this particular stock and move onto the next.

In any case, we'll continue taking the stock through the rest of our due diligence process to see the overall outcome.

#2 - The Quickview

1. *Is a moat present?*

No. I would argue that coffee is a pretty commoditized business, so it is challenging to build up a competitive moat around and within this industry.

In my area of the world, two main coffee companies exist: Caribou and Starbucks. Both have good coffee and both are equally as popular. The issue as I see it is that all things being considered, very few people that I know must have only one particular brand of coffee. Individuals then choose what is most convenient - often times using closeness of the coffee shop as the deciding factor.

While coffee is a commodity, the service and scale behind that coffee could be construed as a competitive advantage. The sheer size of Starbucks makes it quite the entity for other coffee companies to compete against.

The size and reach of the giant certainly offers advantages in the way of economies of scale and better optimization of growing, sourcing, trading etc.

Overall though, I would argue that a strong moat doesn't exist for the coffee giant. Anyone can get into the coffee industry so long as they can purchase and own a storefront. I don't see this as a huge negative for the company, I just acknowledge that selling a particular type of coffee is not a competitive advantage.

2. Is the CFFO positive?

Yes. Cash flow for the quarter end was $4B, which is solid to see. This stems from a combination of sold net income, a large depreciation expense, and what looks to be cash flow saved through having sold operations and not incurring certain expenditures into the future.

When I do a quick look I see much of the same; solid, positive operating cash flows for the past few years and quarters.

3. Did CFFO cover dividend payments?

Yes. At nearly $4B for the quarter-end, SBUX shows that it is able to generate a solid cash flow from operations, more than enough to cover the dividend payments of $1.3B

Even with CAPEX added back in of $1.3B, the company still cash flowed.

This type of cash-generation power shows me that the company earns solid cash, day-in and day-out.

4. Was working capital positive the past three years?

Yes. Working capital has been positive for the past three years, and the trend towards more positive working capital is growing. In 2016, the company's working capital was $210mm (1.05x), which is very thin for a company of Starbucks size.

However, in 2018, that number shows it has jumped to $6.81B (2.2x). This is the type of growth that I like to see. The only large question is, will it be continued into the future? Time will tell.

5. Is the company in a growing industry?

Yes. The coffee sector is growing at a fast pace right now, with seemingly every company looking to get a position in some way or some form. I believe that companies that are well positioned to take advantage of this trend will be beneficiaries in the years to come.

This is where Starbucks has a great presence. Their stores are always busy as people love their coffee. I like the long-term prospects for their positioning world-wide coffee scene.

6. Is the debt/equity at, close to, or under 1x?

No. Debt/Equity is currently negative as Starbucks has a negative equity position, which means that the debt/equity is higher than normal because no equity exists. This is typically a red-flag situation for investors, but considering the stock is performing well, I am not very concerned as to this situation.

In reviewing the Starbucks consolidated statements of equity, we can see that the reason for the large negative equity position is due to the fact that the company has been making aggressive share repurchases in the past few years, to the tune of $8B worth as of 6/30/19.

By making these share repurchases, the company has been increasing shareholder value while negatively affecting the equity base. A combination of cash and long-term debt has been used to buy up these shares. For the everyday shareholder, this is a net positive as the share price will increase as more shares are bought.

So long as the company continues its solid cash flow and we operate in a low-interest rate environment, I do not see this as an issue for SBUX.

#3 - The Spread

Next we'll move onto The Spread. Here we will review the 6/30/19 3 mo. #s.

High-Level Summary Information

	6/30/2019	9 mos.
High Level #s		
P/E Ratio		34.17
MC		112,709,524,383
Equity		(4,319,000,000)
P/B		(26.10)
Liabilities		25,213,000,000
Debt/Equity		(5.84)
Debt/BV		(2.89)
Working Capital		1,839,000,000
Working Capital Ratio		1.31

The High-Level Summary Section Highlights:

- The PE Ratio is very high at the moment. This means that investors are paying more per share for each dollar of income the company generates. We typically want to see this sub 20x to consider a stock at a ripe entry point.

- Equity is negative. Normally this means the stock is incurring losses year-over-year and is a cause for concern. However, as discussed above, SBUX is currently engaging in an aggressive share buyback program, which has been depleting equity through utilizing cash and incurring debt.

- Working capital is solid.

The Balance Sheet

Balance Sheet

Current Assets	7,735,000,000
Cash, A/R	4,763,000,000
PPE	6,188,000,000
Total Assets	20,894,000,000
Current Liabilities	5,896,000,000
Long-term Liabilities	19,317,000,000
Total Liabilities	25,213,000,000
Equity	(4,319,000,000)
Intangible Assets	4,418,000,000
Book Value	(8,737,000,000)
Working Capital	1,839,000,000
Working Capital ratio	1.31
Debt/Equity ratio	(5.84)
Debt/BV	(2.89)

Balance Sheet Highlights:

● The cash position is solid at $5B.

● Current assets are covering current liabilities, which is what investors always want to see.

● Book value is negative when we add back in the intangible assets. This will be something we want to take a look at when we take this stock into the Deep Dive process.

141

The Income Statement

Income Statement

Sales	19,762,000,000
COGS	16,973,000,000
Gross Profit	2,789,000,000
Interest Expense	253,000,000
Net Income	2,796,000,000
Depreciation & Amortization	1,033,000,000
Taxes	670,000,000
EBITDA	4,752,000,000
Profit Margin	14.15%
EBITDA/Int Exp	18.78
NI/Int Exp	11.05

Income Statement Highlights:

- The income statement is rock solid. Overall this is the type of income statement that an investor would like to see.

- Interest expense is covered nicely at 11x. This tells me that the company can service its debt adequately.

- Solid profit margins, net income, and EBITDA.

The Cash Flow Statement

Cash Flow Statement

CFFO	3,939,000,000
CFFI	(507,000,000)
CFFF	(7,423,000,000)
Change in Cash	(3,991,000,000)
Divs	1,331,000,000
CFFO/Divs	2.96

Cash Flow Highlights:

- Solid CFFO, which is the most important metric for a dividend investor.

- CFFO covers dividends at 3x, which is a good ratio.

- Cash flow from financing activities is a bit higher than I'd like to see at ($7.4B). This will be something for to dig into in the Deep Dive to understand why and how the company took on so much financing for daily operations.

The Spread Summary: SBUX

Overall Starbucks is a stock on solid footing. It is cash flow positive, which is ideally what dividend investors want to see when considering investing in a dividend-paying stock.

However, the stock price has been on an upward run of late, which has SBUX trading close to 52 week highs.

If I were to look at initiating a position in this stock in this present day, I would most likely hold off on deploying capital as the stock is overpriced from a dividend payment perspective. There would be a good chance to consider investing should the dividend be increased, if a split occurs, or if the stock trends downward.

For now though, SBUX is a bit too rich for the consideration of additional shares.

AT&T ($T) Dividend Analysis

AT&T is an interesting stock; it is a long-term communications company that is making a foray into the world of content. With the acquisition of Turner Network Television (TNT), it delved into a vast array of viewable programs which it is hoping to leverage across its multitude of current communications customers.

AT&T happens to be the highest dividend paying stock currently in my portfolio. So would I buy this stock today? Let's go through the process.

#1 - Forward Dividend Income

The first item I look at when considering investing in a stock is, "what is the forward dividend income?"

At today's price of $34.82, the $T analysis comes up with the following data points:

Forward Dividend Calculator

Investment Amount	$5,000.00
Stock Ticker	T
Company	AT&T
Share Price	$34.82
Dividend	$0.51
Dividend Frequency	4
Annual Dividend Payout	$2.04
Shares Purchased	143.6
Payout/Yr.	$292.94
Payout/Qtr.	$73.23
Yield	5.86%
Share Accumulation	8.41

At a $5,000 investment level, I like the fact that we could add $292.94 in forward dividend income while accumulating approximately 8-9 extra shares per year via having this position on DRIP.

Remember that one of the big things that we are looking for

is share accumulation. The quicker we can build up our share count, the more dividend income we will receive. All else being equal, I would favor a lower priced stock over a higher priced stock as the lower price point allows me to accumulate shares much faster.

DivTalk: If you want to do your own Forward Dividend Income calculation, head on over to https://www.moneybyramey.com/dividend-income-calculator/, where I built out a forward dividend income calculator for you to use in your journey towards building your dividend income!

Because I can accumulate a multitude of shares and receive an adequate amount of dividend income, I am further intrigued by this stock's potential. Since it passes the forward dividend income test, we'll head on over to the QuickView phase.

#2 - The QuickView

In the QuickView step, we'll go back to our previously discussed criteria to answer the following questions:

1. *Is a moat present?*

Yes. The telecommunications industry is highly commoditized. People do not really care where they get their internet from, so long as they do get their internet. I'm sure you have people who go with a carrier because they believe it is the best one out there, but by-and-large, most people want the best price possible. In general, it is a race to the bottom and not conducive to a well developed moat discussed in Michael Porter's Five Forces analysis.

However, being that AT&T has 370 million customers and has recently made a foray deeper into the world of content via buying Time Warner, I believe that the sheer size and delivery network available to AT&T makes it very tough, if not impossible, to duplicate.

In addition to having a vast number of customers, it is now able to deliver more content to those customers. I believe that the future of these companies will be highly dependent on who makes the mark in the field of content creation. AT&T has a leg up in the two areas of a massive user base and a great content creation system.

2. Was the Cash Flow From Operations positive?

Yes. Cash Flow From Operations was positive for the most recently available data. The 3/31/19 numbers show that CFFO was a healthy $11B dollars. I like to see positive numbers as this indicates that at the end of the day, the company made real, cold hard cash.

As an investor, this is very important to see, as AT&T needs to be able to generate adequate cash flow in order to service its daily expenses and debt load.

3. Did CFFO cover dividend payments?

Yes. The dividend payment was covered by the CFFO. The total dividend payment was $3.7B in 3/31/19 Q1, which meant that AT&T paid $3.7B to all common shareholders. Each shareholder received a dividend payout of $.51 cents per share.

Being that AT&T made $11B in cash flow, the dividend was covered adequately.

4. *Was there positive working capital the past three years?*

No. Unfortunately, AT&T is operating at a working capital deficit, which means that it owes more current debt due than it has liquid assets available to pay those debts.

This can be a challenging situation for a company to find itself in as this means if all current liabilities needed to be paid immediately, then the company would not have enough current assets to do so. It would either need to borrow money or raise equity.

This metric usually is an indication of a company's overall cash management strategy. While I do not want to see a company holding a large cash position unnecessarily, a positive working capital cushion tells me that the company is flush with cash needed to run its operations and that overall, the company is on solid financial footing. Anything otherwise could spell troubling times when hard economic times hit and sources of financing dry up.

5. *Is the company in a growing industry?*

Yes/No. This is a subjective measurement though and one that requires a bit of explaining. Overall, AT&T is growing. It is moving into content and wireless, which I do not see going away any time soon. It is making inroads to 5G technology and is here to continue servicing a growing mobile base.

However, it is also involved in legacy services, such as landline telephone, which will be dead in 10 years time. One could also make the argument that DirectTV will have declines as more and more houses are connected with higher speed internet to stream their favorite shows. Cord cutting is real.

Overall though, I see AT&T having nice cash flow which comes from servicing a solid customer base in the technology sector, so I am willing to predict its future growth prospects are good.

6. *Is the debt/equity at, close to, or under 1x?*

No. This is where AT&T takes the biggest hit. To continue life in the telecommunications sector, companies need to use their capital to maintain their equipment, properties, and technology infrastructure. This is often referred to as CAPEX.

$T not only needs to spend a good amount of its earnings to keep up with CAPEX, but it has also been pivoting into the world content though the Time Warner acquisition. This purchase cost the company $85B in additional debt (4).

The debt/equity ratio for $T now rests at 1.81x. However, when we back out the intangible assets of $172B, the debt/book value ratio skyrockets to 14.88x.

The high debt ratio is one of the reasons why the market doesn't consider $T a slam dunk investment in many analyst's books. It is yet to be determined how successfully the acquisition of Time Warner goes for AT&T, especially considering that the company incurred so much debt to make the deal happen.

The Quickview Results

In my estimation, $T hits on 4/6 quick view categories. For me, this will be enough to take the stock to the next level, into the spread.

#3 - The Spread

In the spread, we are looking to get better insight into the company's numbers. We do this by inputting our numbers in to a predefined template, which will return a few ratios and calculations to give us a bit more insight than the Quickview phase.

Keep in mind that the purpose of the Quickview is an initial glance into whether or not we would want to take the stock into The Spread, The Deep Dive, and eventually, a Buy decisions.

While the Quickview should only take a few minutes to complete, the spread will require you to download the company's most recent financial statements and input numbers into a spreadsheet or other calculation software.

DivTalk: The terminology "The Spread" came about from the fact that in this phase of our investment analysis, we will enter the stocks numbers into a system to get our ratios, calculations and overall summary. When I enter this phase, I do so in a spreadsheet template. Thus, the terminology, "The Spread" was born.

While The Spread is a more thorough look into a stock that the Quickview, the spirit during this process is to continue maintaining a high-level approach to analyzing the stock. The overarching goal of The Spread is to ascertain whether or not you want to take the stock to the next level and complete the Deep Dive Analysis.

The Spread: $T

The first and foremost step in the spread is to enter the data from the latest 10-K or 10-Q into our spreadsheet.

Below is The Spread information for AT&T:

High-Level Summary #s

	3/31/2019	3 mos.
High Level #s		
P/E Ratio		9.07
MC		$274,597,073,379
Equity		194,915,000,000
P/B		1.41
Liabilities		353,433,000,000
Debt/Equity		1.81
Debt/BV		14.88
Working Capital		(18,180,000,000)
Working Capital Ratio		0.72

High-Level Summary Section Highlights:

- The Price/Book ratio of 1.4x tells me that the market is valuing this company at near its equity value. As a value investor, this can be a good indicator that the company is at a good level for investment.

- Negative working capital is noticeable and something I do not like to see. It is concerning and it should be reviewed in the deep dive.

- The debt/equity is manageable, but the debt/BV is very high at 15x. This tells me the company has a lot of intangible assets that are being subtracted from equity. We will need to review the veracity of the intangible assets in the deep dive process to ensure that the company has been making solid acquisitions at good price points

---

DivTalk: It's been in the news quite a bit lately - companies taking massive write downs to the intangible assets on the balance sheet. While these are non-cash expenses from the write-down perspective, they are a very real expense in the company's day-to-day operations.

A write down of these assets - whether a customer list, subsidiary valuation, etc. - represents the fact that the value of these assets has lowered and, more than likely, that the company overpaid for these assets. Both situations are causes for concern and need to be evaluated in depth.

The Balance Sheet

Balance Sheet

Current Assets	46,472,000,000
Cash, A/R	6,516,000,000
PPE	132,051,000,000
Total Assets	548,348,000,000
Current Liabilities	64,652,000,000
Long-term Liabilities	288,781,000,000
Total Liabilities	353,433,000,000
Equity	194,915,000,000
Intangible Assets	171,166,000,000
Book Value	23,749,000,000
Working Capital	(18,180,000,000)
Working Capital ratio	0.72
Debt/Equity ratio	1.81
Debt/BV	14.88

Balance Sheet Highlights:

- AT&T is a massive company. This can be seen in the $548B worth of assets under management. With an ultimate customer base of 370M, it is no surprise that such a large entity needs to exist to service all of those customers (5).

- We will need to dig into the debt situation in more detail when we complete the Deep Dive process.

The Income Statement

Income Statement

Sales	19,762,000,000
COGS	16,973,000,000
Gross Profit	2,789,000,000
Interest Expense	253,000,000
Net Income	2,796,000,000
Depreciation & Amortization	1,033,000,000
Taxes	670,000,000
EBITDA	4,752,000,000
Profit Margin	14.15%
EBITDA/Int Exp	18.78
NI/Int Exp	11.05

Income Statement Highlights:

- $T had solid net income at $2.8B. It has great overall profitability which are reflected in the net income and EBITDA numbers.

- Interest expense is well covered. The biggest cause for concern for AT&T is its massive debt load, which was only increased by acquiring Time Warner.

155

However, with the interest currently being covered well, I do not see the increase in the debt position as a high concern item, so long as AT&T continues with its aggressive debt pay down program.

The Cash Flow Statement

Cash Flow Statement

CFFO	3,939,000,000
CFFI	(507,000,000)
CFFF	(7,423,000,000)
Change in Cash	(3,991,000,000)
Divs	1,331,000,000
CFFO/Divs	2.96

Cash Flow Statement Highlights:

- T is a cash generation machine. In looking at this quarter and its previous quarterly and yearly financials, AT&T does one thing very well; it generates a tremendous amount of cash from operations.

- Dividends are covered adequately at 3x. I would like to see this coverage ratio trend upwards, however with T having such a large share float, it would need to institute a very aggressive share buyback program to help reduce the amount it pays in dividends. I would argue that AT&T is somewhat 'locked' into its dividend payment program, as it has been paying those dividends for 35+ years.

Note: the above data sets come from the financial model I have created in which I enter data from the company's earnings reports. Look for these financial models to be available on MoneyByRamey.com in the coming months ahead.

DivTalk: There are two main forms through which publicly traded companies report their numbers: the Annual Report (10-K) and the Quarterly Report (10-Q). Firms located in the United States are currently required to produce four, unaudited quarterly reports and one, audited annual report per year. These are more commonly referred to as earnings reports.

For the investor, the Annual Report is the one-stop shop where we can find the most information available. The only drawback is that it is only produced once a year.

Therefore I find that the quarterly report is a solid place to keep track of results during the year. Though I will utilize this data in my analysis, I typically like to deep dive on yearly financials as:

1. The 10Ks are audited where as 10Qs typically are unaudited.

2. Quarterly financials can be subjected to cyclical business conditions. Reviewing the 10K helps to 'normalize' the company's trend over a one year time period.

The Spread Summary: $T

Remember that in this Spread process, the goal is not a deep look into the company's overall financial situation, but rather a 50,000 foot glimpse to see if anything glaring happens to stick out that would negatively impact this company and ergo, our investment.

After we enter our numbers into the Spread and start to review the data, the biggest question we want to answer ourselves is whether or not we want to continue this process into The Deep Dive.

If the answer is no, we do not want to go into the Deep Dive, we can stop our analysis and move onto the next stock.

If the answer is yes, we want to complete The Deep Dive, then it is time to move onto The Deep Dive process.

In reviewing T's number spread, the results are somewhat mixed. What stands out is we see a company that generates tons of cash flow, has good interest coverage, but does have a large debt position that could negatively impact future operations.

Combine all of this with its 'locked' dividend payment policy, and we have a company that will be tough to match current market trends.

However, I do see a bright spot in AT&Ts future. With its acquisition of Time Warner and DirectTV, it began making more inroads into content, where the future of entertainment lies.

This certainly intrigues me, and is enough for me to take AT&T into the Deep Dive process to see if this would be a stock worth including in the MoneyByRamey.com portfolio.

The Deep Dive Analysis

For the Deep Dive analysis process, we will utilize the numbers listed in The Spread to go deeper into how valuable a particular stock happens to be.

We want to make sure we ask and answer the proper questions in order to understand the stock in enough depth to make the ultimate decision of whether or not to deploy our hard-earned capital into this particular security.

In the previous section, we outlined a multitude of questions you can ask in an effort to better understand the company's overall financial situation. Keep in mind that we do not have to ask every single question on each stock, but only the ones that will be applicable to the particular analysis at hand.

Below is a list of questions I chose to ask and answer with regards to AT&T.

What is the Company's Valuation?

To ascertain the company's valuation, we'll begin by reviewing the high-level numbers:

3/31/2019	3 mos.
High Level #s	
P/E Ratio	9.07
MC	$278,323,631,114
Equity	194,915,000,000
P/B	1.43
Liabilities	353,433,000,000
Debt/Equity	1.81
Debt/BV	14.88
Working Capital	(18,180,000,000)
Working Capital Ratio	0.72

We can see that $T is trading at an attractive 9.07x PE ratio. This is a good sign as I typically look to invest in any company trading at PE ratio 20x or below.

Secondly, we see that the Price/Book ratio is 1.21x. Price/Book (Market Cap / Equity) tells us how valuable the market believes that the stock actually is. In this case, the market cap for $T is $236B while the entire equity basis is $195B.

This tells us that the market values the stock at nearly what the total equity of the company happens to be. This is important because it shows us that AT&T is trading at an attractive valuation. Typically I like to see P/B ratios trading at lower multiples as this shows that the stock is fairly priced when compared to the underlying assets. However, to confirm this, we'll need to ensure that we take a deep dive into the asset base as well.

Another valuation metric that we can utilize is how valuable the market feels the AT&T customer happens to be. At 159M current users (6), I believe the market is undervaluing this behemoth and the massive potential behind this user base, especially with $T making a foray into the world of content.

Debt Analysis

The next step in The Spread is the debt analysis. For this, we'll bring back in the snippet of AT&T's balance sheet.

Balance Sheet

Current Assets	46,472,000,000
Cash, A/R	6,516,000,000
PPE	132,051,000,000
Total Assets	548,348,000,000
Current Liabilities	64,652,000,000
Long-term Liabilities	288,781,000,000
Total Liabilities	353,433,000,000
Equity	194,915,000,000
Intangible Assets	171,166,000,000
Book Value	23,749,000,000
Working Capital	(18,180,000,000)
Working Capital ratio	0.72
Debt/Equity ratio	1.81
Debt/BV	14.88

This is where AT&T struggles. Though it has a massive equity base of $194.9B, much of this is made up of $171.2B of intangible assets. This means that the company has a book value of only $23.7B.

DivTalk: The goal of the book value is to show the true, tangible assets owned by the company. Book value is calculated by taking assets minus intangible assets. By removing intangible assets, investors can get a better sense

162

of the company's total physical assets.

The differentiation between tangible vs. Intangible assets is important because while both are assets in the true assets in every sense of the word, often times tangible assets are more attractive to investors because the underlying value is easier to judge.

Take for instance the tangible assets of Accounts Receiveable – or assets due from product sold. It is very easy to ascertain this value, account for it on the balance sheet, and value it as an investor. It is simple the amount of widgets sold times the price the widgets were sold at.

On the other side of the spectrum, the value of a customer list, which is an intangible asset, is much more harder for investors to place a proper value upon. What weight should the company give to each customer on the list and the list as a whole? As we've seen with recent intangible asset write downs at General Electric ($GE) and Kraft-Heinz ($KHC), it is quite challenging

Having such high levels of intangible assets makes sense as most of $T's current value is built into its large customer base and the content it delivers to its network. Most of these assets are intangible in nature, meaning they cannot be owned like property can.

DivTalk (A bit more on intangible assets): Intangible assets are those assets for which there is no associated property, plant or equipment. A real life everyday example: the car that you own is a 'tangible' asset in the fact that it is a real, physical thing. However, if you have a customer list that you have built up for your business, then that list has 'intangible' value because it is not a hard, physical asset.

Both assets are very real to the everyday investor, and both assets can gain or lose value over time. As an investor, I typically back out the intangible assets to know the real worth of a company from a PPE perspective.

But keep in mind, intangible assets are just as real as tangible assets. In the case of high levels of intangible assets, how the company values those assets becomes a metric of prime importance.

Why am I discussing tangible vs. intangible assets in a debt analysis? To ensure that we understand how the debt picture affects the company's overall operations.

AT&T's long-term liabilities are at a massive $289B. Even though the company is committed to paying this down as quickly as possible, it is a number that is scaring away many would-be investors. A typical knock on the stock is that investors fear that AT&T's debt will not be serviceable, especially if DirectTV and other services begin to decline in subscriber base.

When looking at the debt, I like to get a sense of how much of a risk that lenders view the property. One way that I accomplish this is to see what interest rate lenders charge to the company.

Though we can ultimately gain more information through the company's 10-K, we can still find good information in the company's quarterly reports. In the most recent AT&T quarterly report, the company had relatively low interest rates:

Our weighted average interest rate of our entire long-term debt portfolio, including the impact of derivatives, was approximately 4.4% as of March 31, 2019 and December 31, 2018. We had $170,532 of total notes and debentures outstanding at March 31, 2019, which included Euro, British pound sterling, Swiss franc, Brazilian real, Mexican peso, Canadian dollar and Australian dollar denominated debt that totaled approximately $41,061.

At March 31, 2019, we had $11,538 of debt maturing within one year, including $2,957 of commercial paper borrowings and $8,441 of long-term debt issuances. Debt maturing within one year includes the following notes that may be put back to us by the holders
- $1,000 of annual put reset securities issued by BellSouth that may be put back to us each April until maturity in 2021
- An accreting zero-coupon note that may be redeemed each May until maturity in 2022. If the remainder of the zero-coupon note (issued for principal of $500 in 2007 and partially exchanged in the 2017 debt exchange offers) is held to maturity, the redemption amount will be $592.

Though not much detail is provided as in the 10-K annual report, the company did disclose that the average weighted interest rate of the long-term debt portfolio was 4.4%. This means that the majority of the portfolio's interest rate balances out to 4.4%.

If we happened to see higher interest rates, this would lead us to believe that lenders view debt issuance to AT&T as higher risk than typical offerings. Since the rate is rather typical of where current lending rates happen to be, I see that AT&T is viewed as a normal risk-grade investment, according to the lending institutions.

How Liquid is the Company?

We want to find out how well the company is able to meet its currently due debt obligations with 'quick assets', such as cash, accounts receivables, inventory, etc. For this, we want to refer back to the balance sheet insert above.

$T's current liquidity is somewhat concerning. In reviewing our working capital numbers generated from the balance sheet, the overall working capital position is negative.

Why is this concerning? Let's dig into this a bit further.

How I view working capital is that if all the current debt needed to be paid today, would the company have enough cash and cash equivalents to do so?

If there are enough cash and cash equivalent items to cover the current debt, this tells me the company is in a strong financial position and doesn't necessarily have the need for current borrowings to finance its day-to-day expenses, as it is being financed by its operations.

For companies that pay dividends, having a good working capital position is vital. This is because a dividend is a highly elective payment by the company.

If a company were to run into financial difficulties, you can be sure that cutting the dividend would be one of the first options on the table. For the dividend investor, cutting the dividend is a scenario that we cannot see, as it would go directly against our strategy.

In reviewing the $T stock, the negative working capital position is noted as a negative in my book. It is not an investment deal-breaker, however this now means that I will give the overall debt picture a deeper dive, as how the company is financing this working capital deficit becomes even more important.

More on this in the upcoming cash flow and dividend safety sections.

Is the Company Cash Flowing?

Cash Flow Statement

CFFO	11,052,000,000
CFFI	(5,401,000,000)
CFFF	(4,421,000,000)
Change in Cash	1,230,000,000
Divs	3,714,000,000
CFFO/Divs	2.98

In my humble opinion, the company's cash flow is the most important item to look at when analyzing a stock. This is because while income can be highly manipulated by certain expenses - especially non-cash expenses - cash flow is a more representative indication of how well the company is doing from a day-to-day, cash generation perspective.

Cash flow answers the question: did the company truly cash flow, and if so, how much did it bring in?

After all, Cash is King.

In looking at AT&T's cash flow, I am impressed. For 3/31/19, it generated $11B in cash flow from operations. This means that across all of its divisions, it essentially made $11B when all things are considered.

Sure $T is a large company, so we would expect it to earn a decent income and cash flow. I like seeing such a large cash flow because it tells me that the $3.7B dividend is relatively safe and covered by cash flows. This means that the company won't have to borrow to keep paying its dividend.

Perhaps more importantly, the company is generating the cash that it needs to pay down its massive debt. Certainly $T will be using its generated cash to continue upgrading its networks to 5G and making the necessary CAPEX investments, but since the dividend is covered and enough cash is left over to pay down debt, it is a win-win in my book.

Is the Dividend Safe?

For the last step of The Deep Drive, we'll take a look into the dividend safety criteria. In our initial Quickview phase, we looked at forward dividend income to ensure that we found a good balance of solid dividend yield and initial purchase price. While this is an important step, as investors, we must go deeper to figure out if the yield is sustainable for the long-term.

If we end up buying a stock with too high of a dividend yield, we might be at risk of a dividend cut as the dividend becomes unsustainable due to the declining business environment or other factors which drive down the company's cash flow.

If we buy too low of yield, I would argue that we're buying into a stock that is not properly valued for investment at the present time, especially in regards to a dividend investing strategy that puts high emphasis on share accumulation.

In this deep dive step, we are now more interested in seeing the relatively safety of the dividend. To complete this phase, there are a few questions we will ask and answer:

Are Dividends Covered By CFFO?

Yes. At $11B in CFFO and $3.7B in dividends paid for the quarter, the coverage is at 2.98x. I personally like to see anything above 2x as this tells me that the dividend is being covered by the current cash generated from operations.

If dividends are not covered by cash flow, this is a cause for concern as that trend is not sustainable. We'll find that when dividends are not covered by cash flow, this means the company will have to finance the dividend payments elsewhere. This primarily means that debt will need to be issued or additional shares of stocks will need to be issued, which will in turn dilute our ownership position and further.

In the case of issuing debt, the company will be on a self-imploding path. By taking on more debt to finance a policy of paying dividends, the chance that the company will be able to catch up becomes less and less realistic. Each additional debt issuance adds to interest expense, which eats into more cash flow.

If the company is not able to grow its revenues to be able to pay down the debt early, then it is only a matter of time before the company falls on a tough path and needs to cut the dividend. I'd actually argue that in these situations, the company is much better off cutting the dividend and focusing on debt repayments. This is not a good candidate to invest in with our dividend strategy.

In the case of issuing more shares, this will hurt us in two ways.

1. Our ownership position will become diluted.

2. If common shares are issued, the company will now have to pay more dividends across more shares.

Either situation is not tenable for a company that does not have adequate cash flow. This is why a company's ability to generate cash on a day-to-day, quarter-to-quarter basis is so important for its continued existence.

What is the Dividend Safety Score?

In unison with ensuring that the dividend is covered by CFFO, we then want to ascertain the general health of the dividend. There are four main categories that investors will analyze:

1. Relative Yield

2. Consistency

3. Safety

4. Growth

There are paid services that will offer analysis on these points, however I typically do my own analysis and testing on how safe the dividend is based on the four points.

Here is my analysis on how AT&T measures up on the four categories:

- **Relative Yield** - T does have a very attractive dividend yield at 5.37%. Its stock price has been depressed for many years, mainly due to the high amounts of debt that the company has incurred. Investors are still unsure whether AT&T will be able to absorb this debt and continue to generate the type of profits it needs to pay it down adequately. As investors, if we are optimistic that AT&T will be able to pay down the debt, the current high-yield makes this an overall attractive investment.

- **Consistency** - T has been a fairly consistent dividend payer for the past 35 years. I believe the stock gets docked a few points on consistency as it has not always increased its dividend at a steady rate. In the past 10 years, it has kept on a fairly consistent increase of $.01 per year; I believe the market was expecting and wanting more.

- **Safety** - Here again, we see the debt levels come into play and negatively affect the dividend safety. T is in a precarious position right now as it took on a lot of extra debt with the Time Warner acquisition. To help allay fears of debt overwhelming the company, it is now on an aggressive debt repayment plan. Time will tell how well management is able to execute this strategy. The company's CFFO/Div ratio is currently at 3x, though with an overall share float of 7.31B, it is a large amount of dividends to pay across its common shareholders.

- **Growth** - T is currently a dividend champion and has paid a dividend for 35 consecutive years. This speaks to its earning and cash flow power. The growth over recent years has been at a slower clip in previous years, but it is still quite impressive. It is my personal contention that the debt will be paid down, cash flow will remain in tact, and AT&T will remain a solid dividend paying investment for many years to come.

Buy?

Now we are at the truly fun part of the process - do we buy this stock or not? Only your solid investment analysis can give you the proper insight.

Here is where the "rubber truly meets the road" and we must now determine if this stock is worthy of owning in our portfolio.

The key is to not get bogged down in paralysis by analysis, but rather keep the information high level, summarized in nature, and make the buy/pass decision based on the stock health picture determined by our thorough analysis. By doing so, we put ourselves in a better position to act.

For AT&T, my high-level takeaways are:

- The company has great cash flow
- There is a large debt on the books that needs to be paid down
- The company has a huge user base for to capitalize on with future initiatives

The main narrative to the story is that while AT&T is cash flowing enormously, it did take on a huge amount of debt to acquire Time Warner. This is in a push to improve its content offerings across its 370M user base, which, if it accomplishes, can yield amazing dividends down the road.

Will the AT&T strategy play out as expected? To me, the results are in the numbers, and I am buying into their story. In fact, T is currently the largest holding in my portfolio when filtered by annual dividend income.

I am executing the 'buying low and holding' strategy through recurring dividend payments on a dividend reinvestment plan. Each time DRIP takes place, I am buying more of this solid, cash-flow stock as lower price points.

Could I be wrong? Absolutely. But my mind seeks out the long-term benefits. And at only 7.18% of my current 35 position portfolio, if T does end up cutting its dividend or falling by the wayside, I have 34 other awesome companies (and growing daily) there to pick up the slack.

As it currently stands, I feel comfortable with buying into this solid company, at a great price, and holding for the long-term.

Will A Dividend Investing Strategy Work for You?

Having read this book, it is now time to begin asking yourself whether or not a dividend investing strategy might work for you. My hope is that the information is laid out in a succinct manner to help you organize your thoughts in screening, buying, and holding a stock from beginning to end.

I find that for me, a 30 something investor with a long time horizon, a dividend investing strategy is perfectly suited for my current situation. I am prone to ignore short-term market fluctuations in favor of seeking long-term potential, largely ignoring the day-to-day fluctuations in between.

Be sure to check back to www.MoneyByRamey.com for all the latest updates on our dividend portfolio, articles, and much much more! We look to write on any money topic, but our main focus is on developing passive income, especially through dividend income. We are always rolling out more tools to help you in your Financial Freedom Journey, so be sure to stay tuned for all the latest updates.

Thank you again for being a reader of my books. I am humbled by the fact that I can be here, writing for you on a daily basis. Good luck and happy investing! As always, upward and onward towards Financial Freedom!

Glossary

Active Income: income that one trades hours in earning.

Dividend Yield: The percentage an investor will receive in dividend income relative to the current company share price. This is calculated by taking the dividend payout per share dividend by the current share price.

Example: a stock pays a $0.50 dividend per share each quarter (4x), and the current share price is $32. The dividend yield would then be 6.25% (($0.50*4)/$32).

DRIP (Dividend Reinvestment Plan): an automated system in which any dividends you receive are automatically reinvested into the stock that you already own. Similar to Dollar Cost Averaging.

Financial Freedom: the place an individual reaches when, through a solid financial position, work becomes a choice and not a must.

Fractional Ownership: a situation that occurs when one reinvests capital on a DRIP program.

Growth Investing: a certain type of investment strategy which is based on the idea that the investor is looking for companies that will have phenomenal growth prospects. The goal is to have appreciation through capital gains.

Mr. Market: the affectionate term for the general crazy reactions of the stock market as a whole. It is a term invented by master value investor Benjamin Graham, in his 1949 masterpiece, The Intelligent Investor

Passive Income: money that you earn through no active efforts to generate. Aka, money that you make while you sleep.

The Dow Jones Industrial Average (DJIA): more commonly referred to as "The Dow", is a collection of 30 stocks that are traded on the stock exchanges.

Return on Assets (ROA): a profitability calculation which determines how efficiently the firm used its assets. It is calculated by taking Net Income divided by the Total Assets. For instance, if a firm has $10,000,000 in assets, and $1,000,000 in net income, it has a 10% (10,000,000 / 1,000,000) ROA.

Return on Equity (ROE): a profitability calculation which determines how efficiently the company is using its equity. It is calculated by taking the Net Income dividend by the Total Equity.

Return on Investment (ROI): a performance measure used to evaluate the efficiency of a particular investment. It is calculated by the following formula:

ROI = (Current Value of Investment – Cost of the Investment) / Cost of Investment.

For instance, if an investor purchases a stock for $10,000, which then goes up to $15,000, their ROI would be 50%:

($15,000 - $10,000) / $10,000

Value Investing: a type of investment strategy in which the investor is looking for stocks that are adequately valued at current market prices, in which the investor primarily believes that the market is unfairly discounting the actual value of the stock. The idea is to have capital gains realization as well.

Citations

(1) https://www.foxbusiness.com/business-leaders/warren-buffetts-berkshire-hathaway-sitting-on-112-billion-in-cash-he-says

(2) https://www.marketwatch.com/story/more-proof-that-millennials-are-beer-snobs-2019-05-02

(3) https://www.forbes.com/sites/greatspeculations/2018/09/04/why-is-coca-cola-paying-a-hefty-premium-for-costa-coffee/#508573f71643

(4) https://www.forbes.com/sites/natalierobehmed/2016/10/23/what-the-85-billion-att-time-warner-deal-means-for-consumers/#2a246a4c2ea6

(5) https://www.att.com/Common/about_us/pdf/att_btn.pdf

(6) https://about.att.com/newsroom/att_by_the_numbers_q1_2018.html

www.ingramcontent.com/pod-product-compliance
Lightning Source LLC
Chambersburg PA
CBHW030634220526
45463CB00004B/1524